MW00379260

Praise for

THE
WORDS
of GOD

"I don't know where I would be if I didn't have the scriptures to guide my daily life through the pitfalls of political deceptions and traps. My friend Kathleen has beautifully and masterfully given us a book that will strengthen us and help us understand some of the beautiful truths and directions that the Book of Mormon gives us in relationship to the Bible. These two books are for our day to help us face the challenges we have. Kathleen has been given a gift of teaching, and her book, *The Words of God*, will help strengthen our testimonies of the scriptures."

—SYLVIA TENNEY ALLEN, Arizona state senator

"Kathleen Danielsen's passion for teaching our Father's children is only surpassed by her love for our Father and His children."

—JERALD LEWIS, superintendent for Edkey Inc. and former bishop and stake president

THE
WORDS
of GOD

8 CRUCIAL BIBLE THEMES *Supported by* THE BOOK OF MORMON

KATHLEEN DANIELSON

CFI

An imprint of Cedar Fort, Inc.
Springville, Utah

© 2018 Kathleen Danielson
All rights reserved.

No part of this book may be reproduced in any form whatsoever, whether by graphic, visual, electronic, film, microfilm, tape recording, or any other means, without prior written permission of the publisher, except in the case of brief passages embodied in critical reviews and articles.

This is not an official publication of The Church of Jesus Christ of Latter-day Saints. The opinions and views expressed herein belong solely to the author and do not necessarily represent the opinions or views of Cedar Fort, Inc. Permission for the use of sources, graphics, and photos is also solely the responsibility of the author.

ISBN 13: 978-1-4621-2289-9

Published by CFI, an imprint of Cedar Fort, Inc.
2373 W. 700 S., Springville, UT 84663
Distributed by Cedar Fort, Inc., www.cedarfort.com

LIBRARY OF CONGRESS CATALOGING-IN-PUBLICATION DATA

Names: Danielson, Kathleen, 1944- author.
Title: Words of God : 8 crucial Bible themes supported by The Book of Mormon
   / Kathleen Danielson.
Description: Springville, Utah : CFI, an imprint of Cedar Fort, Inc., [2018]
   | Includes bibliographical references.
Identifiers: LCCN 2018016473 | ISBN 9781462122899 (perfect bound : alk. paper)
Subjects: LCSH: Book of Mormon--Relation to the Bible. | Church of Jesus
   Christ of Latter-day Saints--Doctrines. | Mormon Church--Doctrines.
Classification: LCC BX8627 .D365 2018 | DDC 289.3/22--dc23
LC record available at https://lccn.loc.gov/2018016473

Cover design by Shawnda T. Craig
Cover design © 2018 Cedar Fort, Inc.
Edited by Melissa Caldwell and Justin Greer
Typeset by Kaitlin Barwick

Printed in the United States of America

10 9 8 7 6 5 4 3 2 1

Printed on acid-free paper

CONTENTS

One common thread throughout the Bible is the fate of the house of Israel. In this chapter, I discuss the identity of Israel and his family, as well as the blessings of his sons, particularly those of Judah and Joseph, and the implications those blessings have throughout the scriptures and in our lives today. I will follow the thread of Israel throughout the history of God's people. I will then revisit the theme of Israel in the rounding up of the last days in Theme 8.

Covenants are divine promises between God and man. Covenants have existed since Adam. I will differentiate the covenants and the tokens of the covenant. I will discuss why covenants and ordinances are important in the kingdom of God. The covenant is a contract. The ordinance is the signature on the contract, signifying to God that we accept the terms of the covenant. I have come to understand why covenants and ordinances are important to us and to the Lord and why we must pay divine heed to our promises.

In this chapter I will look at the Holy Priesthood after the Order of the Son of God and why it is so important in administering the ordinances of the gospel. I will discuss from the Bible about the lesser priesthood of Aaron, given to the Israelites of the Old Testament. From the Apostle Paul, I will discuss the higher priesthood after the order of Melchizedek. I look at examples from the Bible and the Book of Mormon that show the true power of righteous authority.

The cycle of obedience and disobedience, along with consequences, has existed since Cain. This cycle is seen repeatedly in the Old Testament in the house of Israel, but it is nowhere more apparent than it is among the people of the Book of Mormon. I will discuss examples of individual and group apostasy and the importance of being aware of the role of pride in the downfall of nations. I look at apostasy in the Old and New Testaments and in the Book of Mormon. I look at the influence of anti-Christs in planting the seeds of false doctrine, which lead to apostasy. I discuss in some detail the Great Apostasy and the circumstances that allowed it to occur.

This chapter discusses the Creation and the Fall. God gave mankind his agency in the Garden of Eden. Agency has been an important part of the Father's plan for His children since before the Creation. I discuss the conditions of the Fall and its necessity. I examine why agency is so vital and why there must be opposition in all things. I also discuss the natural consequences of both obedience and disobedience and how all people will ultimately be held accountable for their choices in this life.

In this chapter, I look at Christ's infinite Atonement. I discuss why the Atonement is so vital to God's plan and its necessity for us, as individuals who are hoping to return to God's presence. The Atonement began in the Garden of Gethsemane, as Christ felt the heaviness of the burdens of mankind's sins. It ended on the cross, and all of creation mourned and the earth itself groaned in agony. I also discuss the relationship of love, grace, and works in understanding the value of the Atonement in our individual lives.

In this theme, I discuss the Resurrection of Jesus and why understanding the physical nature of Christ's resurrection helps us understand the Godhead more fully. I look back at the history of the early Church and show how many pure doctrines were changed due to outside influences and philosophies. I will show how Christ's appearance to the Nephites is truly "another testament" of Jesus Christ.

In this chapter, I come full circle from the founding of the house of Israel to the gathering of the house of Israel in the last days. I look at the concluding chapters of the earth through the prophecies of Daniel, Jesus Christ (Joseph Smith—Matthew 24), the Apostle John (Book of Revelation), and the Book of Mormon. We witness the divinity and eternality of Heavenly Father's plan for His children through the Creation and Fall and Christ's infinite

Atonement, death, and Resurrection. Finally, I will contrast the righteous, symbolic bride of Christ with Babylon, the "whore of the earth"; how Babylon will fall; and how Christ will triumph in a glorious millennial reign.

PREFACE

The Beginning of My Journey

I was born during the last year of World War II. My father was stationed in England the night I was born, and he wouldn't know of my safe arrival and Mother's health until several weeks later. At home and abroad, the world had been turned upside down.

When the men came home from the war, they wanted a life that was better for their children. Although that may have happened in terms of material possessions, it was not true in those things that money cannot buy. So much had been changed in American culture since the end of World War II that families moved far from towns that had been home for three or four generations, all the while looking for the American dream. It may have been because of this separation from the support system of extended families and neighborhoods, or it may have been because a huge number of post-war babies were being born (who came to be known as "baby boomers"), but whatever the reason, post-war America began to change. By the end of 1963, the year after I graduated from high school, rock music was king (or in this case, the Beatles), a president was assassinated, and prayer was taken out of the schools. Social mores changed. This change was summed up well in a popular bumper sticker of the '60s: *Sex, Drugs, and Rock 'n' Roll.*

I was a child who watched and listened, and to this day I remember clearly many of the things that I noticed, even though I didn't understand the implications of those things until later in life. One thing I have observed is that there have been significant changes in the role that religion and the Bible play in American life. During the 1950s, most people went to church, at least occasionally. The concept of right and wrong from thousands of years of Judeo-Christian teachings was generally accepted in the home and school and workplace, as well as in the churches. The Bible was accepted as truth, and an appeal to the Bible gave little room for argument. That is far from the case today. The baby boomer generation began tearing down the moral fences that protected honor, truth, and decency without ever giving a single thought to why those fences had been built. Some of those fences needed to come down. Most did not. The world in which I live today is dramatically different from the world in which I grew up.

Desire to Restore Historical Connection

Several years ago, I wrote a document called *With Love and a Challenge: The Book of Mormon and the Bible.* It was the result of years of gospel study of ancient scripture and a desire to help my children and grandchildren see where the Book of Mormon fit in to the historical and doctrinal framework of the Bible.

As I have revisited the work many years later, I find that it not only puts the Book of Mormon into a Biblical perspective, it also puts the Bible into a clearer perspective because of the strength it receives from the Book of Mormon. As stated earlier, people have moved away from the Bible and Biblical teachings. Many of the stories such as the Garden of Eden, the Tower of Babel, and Noah and the Ark have become pure mythology, even to some who consider themselves to be religious, and, yes, even some who are ministers of religion. They see these stories as morality tales, similar to Aesop's Fables, and not as the divine words of patriarchs and prophets. More and more people who accept Jesus at all see Him as a rabbi, a great moral teacher, even a prophet, but not the Son of God. When the Book of Mormon: Another Testament of Jesus Christ is added to the Bible, the truthfulness of doctrines and events becomes manifest.

This confusion became possible because there are so many interpretations and translations of the Bible, many of which contradict one another or present Jesus as less than divine. I once heard someone explain this from the perspective of geometric possibilities. If we have only one point (in this case, the Bible), we can draw an infinite number of lines through that point. The world has been doing that for thousands of years and continues to stray further from God's Word.

The Bible by Itself

However, when you add the Book of Mormon to that picture, it creates a second point of reference. We can only draw one line through two points and, in this case, the line is the pure gospel of Jesus Christ.

The Book of Mormon alongside the Bible

As I revisited the work I wrote for my children and grandchildren, I approached it from a different perspective. I wanted to show how the Old Testament, New Testament, and Book of Mormon fit together both historically and doctrinally. I even touched on some geographical notes as I attempt to place these ancient scriptures side by side in both time and space.

Before my father died, he gave a copy of the Bible and the Book of Mormon to my best friend, who was a member of a different Christian denomination. He promised her that if she would read the Book of Mormon, she would understand the Bible better and become an even better Christian. I believe this to be true.

Please join me on this journey and find out for yourself.

INTRODUCTION TO THE THEMES

The Prophet Ezekiel wrote:

> The word of the Lord came again unto me, saying,
>
> Moreover, thou son of man, take thee one stick, and write upon it, For Judah, and for the children of Israel his companions: then take another stick, and write upon it, For Joseph, the stick of Ephraim, and for all the house of Israel his companions:
>
> And join them one to another into one stick; and they shall become one in thine hand.
>
> And when the children of thy people shall speak unto thee, saying, Wilt thou not shew us what thou meanest by these?
>
> Say unto them, Thus saith the Lord God; Behold, I will take the stick of Joseph, which is in the hand of Ephraim, and the tribes of Israel his fellows, and will put them with him, even with the stick of Judah, and make them one stick, and they shall be one in mine hand. (Ezekiel 37:15–19)

In The Church of Jesus Christ of Latter-day Saints, we have come to know that these passages of Biblical scripture refer to the Bible (the *stick* of Judah) and the Book of Mormon (the *stick* of Ephraim). They also refer to the ultimate gathering and bringing together of two major tribes of Israel, long alienated from one another. The Old Testament covers God's dealing with His people from their beginnings in Genesis until the closing lines of Malachi in about 480 BC. The New Testament begins with the birth of Jesus Christ until John's Revelation around AD 90. There is an intertestamental period of a little over 500 years between the two in which many things occurred that are not included in the Biblical canon. The Book of Mormon basically covers the time between the fall of Jerusalem in about 600 BC and the destruction of the Nephites around AD 480.

I'd like to discuss how both sticks become one in God's hand and how each book supports and testifies of the truthfulness of the other. There are several key themes throughout both books and, using those themes, I hope to tie these books together into a united and cohesive whole.

In 1972, President Marion G. Romney, then a counselor in the First Presidency, was presenting a training for Regional Representatives of The

Church of Jesus Christ of Latter-day Saints. After the conference, as he was walking out, he stopped to speak to Elder Jacob de Jager of the Seventy. President Romney asked how he was going to teach all those inspired materials. In his own words, Elder de Jager shared this experience in General Conference in 1978. Feeling somewhat overwhelmed, he paused to think "of an answer that would satisfy a member of the First Presidency of the Church. [He] replied, 'President Romney, I shall teach in such a way that everyone will *understand.*'

"President Romney, a twinkle in his eye, said, 'That's not enough; you shall teach in such a way that no one will *misunderstand* these divine materials.'"[1]

I remember Elder de Jager's address very well, even though it's been fifty years since I heard it. I have tried to teach the gospel in such a way that people will not just *understand*, but so that no one will *misunderstand*. I have approached this book with that mindset. I hope this will help others to better understand the divine words of prophets, Apostles, and patriarchs.

Note

1.   Jacob de Jager, "Let There Be No Misunderstanding" *Ensign*, November 1978.

The Founding of the House of Israel

The first theme I want to discuss is that of the house of Israel. What is it and why is it important? How does it relate to the Bible? How does it relate to the Book of Mormon? Who was Israel and when do we first hear mention of Father Israel in the scriptures?

Although the house of Israel—past, present, and future—is a uniting theme throughout the Old and New Testament, most Christians give very little thought to its importance. It takes the Book of Mormon, which also carries the same uniting theme, to bring it into focus.

When I study something, it helps me to see the big picture. Otherwise, it's like a 10,000-piece puzzle, the image of which I can't see or understand. I must do the work to put the pieces together into a cohesive whole before the picture becomes clear. I want to do that for you: I want to place these books of ancient scripture in time and space alongside one another. At the same time, I will show how the Bible supports the Book of Mormon and how the Book of Mormon supports the Bible. President Benson wrote that the Book of Mormon "confounds false doctrine and lays down contention."[1] The Bible also supports the Book of Mormon in an understanding of the house of Israel and its place in the history of the world and in the eternal plan of our Heavenly Father.[2] I'll begin my discussion with a historical perspective to both ancient scriptures, the Bible and the Book of Mormon.

I want to jump right into the middle of the story and start with a man well known even by people who do not know the Bible. This young man is so well known because Andrew Lloyd Webber put his name on the marquee![3]

Joseph and His Coat of Many Colors

Thanks to Andrew Lloyd Webber, more people know about Joseph and his coat of many colors through musical theater than through reading Genesis 39 to 50.

Joseph's father was a man named Jacob. God gave Jacob a new name, Israel. He is known most frequently by that name in the scriptures.

Joseph was the eleventh of Jacob's twelve sons. He was also Jacob's favorite, which didn't sit well with his ten older brothers. Joseph had dreams that he shared with his family, concluding that the day would come when all the brothers would all bow down to Joseph. Then Jacob had a coat made for Joseph of many colors in contrast to what must have been plain brown robes of the other sons. Joseph's elder brothers were jealous of him and sought to kill him.

One day, when Joseph took food to his brothers in the fields, they captured him and discussed how best to slay him. His eldest brother, Reuben, stopped them and told them that instead, they should just throw Joseph into a pit, which they did, until they could agree upon what to do with him. As they were eating the lunch Joseph had brought them, they saw a caravan in the distance. These were Ishmaelites[4] on their way to Egypt. Judah, one of the ten, asked the others—what did it profit them to kill Joseph when they could sell him to these traders, who would then take him with them to Egypt? This is what they did. Fearing what their father would say when Joseph wasn't with them, they took his beautiful coat and dipped it in the blood of a young goat they had slain and told Jacob that his beloved son had been killed by a wild beast.

The Ishmaelites sold Joseph to an Egyptian named Potiphar. Because of his honest nature, Joseph was soon in a position of high favor with his master. Due to an accusation of a sin Joseph did not commit, Potiphar had him thrown into prison. There he interpreted the dreams of the royal butler and the royal baker from Pharaoh's court. The butler was released, and the baker was executed, just as Joseph had interpreted from their dreams.

Sometime later, Pharaoh had two disturbing dreams. It was then that the royal butler remembered Joseph. He told Pharaoh of Joseph's gift of interpreting dreams. Pharaoh had Joseph brought from jail, and Joseph interpreted Pharaoh's dreams. His interpretation was that Egypt would have seven years of plenty followed by seven years of famine. Joseph advised Pharaoh to store up Egypt's grain during the plentiful years so that the people might have bread during the lean years. This all came to pass, and in the end, Joseph found favor with Pharaoh and rose to a position of power, second only to Pharaoh himself.

Through his influence, Joseph was able to bring Jacob's entire family to Egypt, which saved them from the famine. At some point after they arrived, Israel grew old and knew he would soon die. Before his death, he blessed his twelve sons as well as Joseph's two sons, Ephraim and Manasseh. Two of those patriarchal blessings are of particular importance in understanding the heritage of the house of Israel.

Judah's blessing, given by his father, Israel:

> The sceptre shall not depart from Judah, nor a lawgiver from between his feet until Shiloah come; and unto him shall the gathering of the people be. (Genesis 49:10)

Judah, therefore, was promised that kings would come from his line and would reign over the house of Israel until the ultimate King, the Messiah, who would be born of Judah's descendants. The name *Shiloah* comes from the same root word as the Hebrew word *shalom*, which means *peace*. *Shiloah* was to be the *Prince of Peace*, a title consistently attributed to Jesus Christ.

Joseph's blessing, given by his father, Israel:

> Joseph is a fruitful bough, even a fruitful bough by a well; whose branches run over the wall:
>
> . . . the arms of his hands were made strong by the hands of the mighty God of Jacob. . . .
>
> Even by the God of thy father, who shall help thee; and by the Almighty, who shall bless thee with blessing of heaven. . . .
>
> The blessings of thy father have prevailed above the blessings of my progenitors [Isaac and Abraham] unto the utmost bound of the everlasting hills: they shall be on the head of Joseph, and on the crown of the head of him that was separate from his brethren. (Genesis 49:22, 24–26)

Joseph, therefore, was to be separated from his brothers as he had been in Egypt. This occurred around 700 BC when Joseph's progeny were taken away and lost to the pages of history. Despite this, the blessings sealed upon Joseph's head were beyond even those promises given to Abraham and Issac. The seed of Joseph have a great mission to perform in the last days. Remember these blessings, because they are important and will be discussed in more detail later. They are key in discovering the fate of the house of Israel in the Bible and the Book of Mormon. We will see the thread of Israel from the days of Joseph and his brothers through the prophecies of the last days prior to the Second Coming of Jesus Christ.

Moses and the Law

After Joseph's death, pharoahs rose to power who did not like the idea of so many Israelites in Egypt, and therefore they set them at hard labor for hundreds of years (Exodus 1:8–11). There was a prophecy in the land that one day a deliverer would be born who would free the Children of Israel from their Egyptian bondage. In response, and out of fear, Pharoah passed a law calling for the midwives in Goshen[5] to report any male child delivered to an Israelite mother. These children were then to be thrown into the Nile River.

The midwives did not do Pharoah's bidding. Whenever they could, they would tell the Egyptian overseers that the Hebrew women were hardier than the Egyptian women and delivered themselves before the midwives could arrive. The parents would then hide their male children as long as they could.

One such family was of the tribe of Levi. A son was born into their home. When the baby was three months old, his mother wrapped him in a blanket and placed him in a covered basket woven of bullrushes made waterproof with a coating of pitch. She set him adrift on the Nile and sent her daughter to watch what happened.

That day, the pharoah's daughter was bathing in the Nile with her hand-maidens when she saw the tiny ark caught in the bullrushes. She rescued the baby and adopted him as her own son, naming him Moses because he was drawn from the water.

Moses was raised as a prince in Egypt until the day he saw an Egyptian beating a Hebrew slave. Moses killed the Egyptian and buried his body in the sand. When this was discovered, Moses was banned from Egypt and set outside the borders of the land in what was then the land of Canaan and the Sinai Desert.

There Moses was taken in by a tribe of Midianites and was adopted by the sheik or priest of the Midianites, a man named Jethro. Moses married Jethro's daughter and stayed on in Midian as a shepherd for many years.

One day, while watching his flock, Moses saw a light on the side of Mount Horeb. On further investigation, he saw that there was a bush that looked to be burning and yet was not consumed. Then Moses heard a voice from within the bush; he was shaken, physically and emotionally. He was told to take off his shoes because he was on holy ground. That voice was the Voice of the Lord,[6] the great I AM. Moses was shown and taught many things, among which was the fact that he himself was the promised deliverer whose life had been spared for just this mission. Moses was hesitant, feeling inadequate in his speech, so the Lord gave to him his elder brother Aaron to be his spokesperson.

They traveled to Egypt and received audience with Pharoah. After many disappointments, miracles, and curses, Pharoah finally relented and told Moses to take the Israelites and leave Egypt forever. After Moses and his people left, Pharoah had a change of heart and sent his army and chariots after the fleeing band. The people were trapped between Pharoah's army and the sea. Through a great miracle, Moses, with the power of God behind him, was able to part the Red Sea so that the Children of Israel could cross on dry ground. When the army tried to follow, the sea closed in on them and they were drowned.

But it wasn't as easy as all that. They were free *from* Egypt, but they weren't free *of* Egypt. After hundreds of years of slavery in a land of idols that were worshipped as gods, the Children of Israel found it difficult to break loose from the influence and tradition of multiple gods. While Moses was on Mount Sinai receiving God's law for Israel, the people—including Moses's brother Aaron and sister Miriam—were gathering their gold to melt down and form a golden calf. Not only did the people bow down to the calf, but they also made a sacrifice on an altar before it and began to sing and dance and do sinful things before God.

When Moses came down from the mountain and saw what was happening, he broke the tablets of God's law. When he later returned to the mountain, he received a lesser law, which we have come to know as the Law of Moses. Because of this and many other instances of moaning, complaining, and rejection of the Lord, the Children of Israel were cursed to wander through the wilderness for forty years. Almost the entire population of people who had left Egypt as adults had to die before God would lead them into the land He had promised their forefathers.

Each of the tribes of Israel was given a land inheritance, with one exception: the tribe of Levi, Moses's own tribe. The Levites were called to be the religious leaders in Israel, and they were given inheritance among all the tribes, sprinkled among them to administer the ordinances of the lesser law and the lesser or Levitical priesthood. Those who were literal descendants of Aaron were to serve as the priests while other Levites served in other ecclesiastical callings under the Law of Moses. Joseph's inheritance was given to his two sons, Ephraim and Manasseh, thus creating the *Twelve Tribes of Israel*.

In the beginning, the Israelites existed as a confederation of tribes governed by judges. They had wars and disputes with their neighbors, sometimes winning and sometimes losing, but they were not a great military or political power in the Middle East. From the very beginning, Israel was plagued by a desire to be like her neighbors. Those nations had kings; because the Lord was Israel's king, she did not have a mortal king. Instead, God gave her a system of judges. The other nations were polytheistic, worshipping many gods and goddesses; Israel was montheistic, the only nation on the face of the earth, at that point in history, to worship one God and one God only. Other nations made images of their gods; Israel was specifically commanded not to do so. Their tendency to yearn after pagan gods was a temptation from the beginning and eventually led to the downfall of God's people.

Despite God's warning about the dangers of having a king and putting that much power into the hands of one man, the people grew dissatisfied with judges. Soon the Israelites began to petition God through the Prophet Samuel to give them a king like their neighbors. Samuel warned them that this was not God's plan for them and that they would live to regret it. They continued to implore Samuel to plead with God for a king. God reluctantly gave them a gentle young man named Saul to be their first king. King Saul began his rule as a very good man, but power corrupts, and it corrupted Saul and ultimately drove him mad. The throne was taken from Saul and given to a young man named David of the tribe of Judah.

David and Solomon

David was a young shepherd boy of no consequence when he was chosen by God through His prophet Samuel to be the king to succeed Saul. In the beginning, even Samuel questioned God's judgment, but he was told:

> Look not on his countenance, or on the height of his stature; because I have refused him: for the Lord seeth not as man seeth; for man looketh on the outward appearance, but the Lord looketh on the heart. (1 Samuel 16:7)

But, like Saul, David also fell from grace. It began one evening when David was walking on his rooftop balcony and he saw a young woman bathing on the rooftop of her home across from the palace. Bathsheba was beautiful, although married, and David was drawn to her. Instead of averting his eyes, he continued to gaze at her until his lustful desire to possess her became almost overwhelming. He sent for her and the two committed adultery.

When Bathsheba became pregnant, David panicked. Her husband, Uriah, was away fighting one of Israel's many wars. Once the pregnancy become obvious, everyone would know that the child could not be Uriah's. The penalty for adultery in Israel was death, usually by stoning.

David sent for Uriah to return home on leave, hoping that Uriah would then sleep with his wife so that she could claim the child was her husband's. But Uriah was so dedicated to his king that he refused to go home; he slept, instead, at the palace. David must have been frantic because he then compounded his original sin with one even more grievous sin. He ordered Uriah back to the battlefield and told his commander to place Uriah on the front lines and make sure that he was killed.

After Uriah's death, David married Bathsheba. I don't know if the people of the kingdom were fooled, but God certainly wasn't.[7] The Lord sent the Prophet Nathan to confront David with his sins. He did so by telling David a parable in which David himself named his own condemnation. This parable opened the king's eyes and wiped away any rationalization David may have had about the severity of his sin. He wept and grieved and was truly penitent, but the damage was done. A little boy was born to David and his new wife, but the child only lived a short while before dying. David was inconsolable. Later, he and Bathsheba would have another son, whom they named Solomon.

Upon David's death, Solomon became king. He was very young and more than a little apprehensive about taking on this huge responsibility. To his credit, he did not pray for riches nor power, but to have an understanding heart. As a result of his humble plea, God granted him all three: riches, power, and wisdom. God allowed Solomon to build His temple in Jerusalem, which he had forbidden David to do, because David had blood on his hands.

Under Kings David and Solomon, the nation of Israel became a force to be reckoned with in the area. David was known for his great military prowess and he increased the territory held by Israel and kept her borders safe. Solomon was recognized throughout the known world for his wisdom and his riches. Even today, Jews look back on the reigns of David and Solomon as the golden age for the Children of Israel.

Political and Religious
Civil War—Two Kingdoms

Unfortunately, Solomon also fell. He had taken many wives from among his pagan neighbors in political alliances and had allowed his wives to bring their foreign gods into Israel, including placing their god images in the temple. Soon the entire kingdom was infected with a growing apostasy. He also taxed his people heavily to support his wives and concubines, which bred discontent, even among his own children and his advisors.

After Solomon's death about 950 BC, Israel experienced civil war. Rehoboam, the rightful heir as a son of Solomon, took his father's throne. He was young and immature, a weak leader who followed unwise counsel. The elderly advisors of Solomon petitioned Rehoboam to take away the unrealistic tax burdens placed on the kingdom by his father in his dotage. They said that would show him to be a just and fair ruler in the eyes of the people. His brash young advisors told him to keep laws in place and even add to the burdens so that he could show the country that he was a strong leader who could not be intimidated. Unfortunately, he followed his young advisors.

This led to a revolt. A man from the tribe of Ephraim, Jeroboam, led a fight against Rehoboam, the tribe of Judah, and the descendants of David.

Jeroboam based his campaign on the wickedness of David's natural heir and on the crushing taxes ordered by Solomon. As soon as the kingdoms were separated, Jeroboam showed himself to be even more unrighteous than his rival by setting up idols in his kingdom. Two of these idols were golden calves that were supposed to be images of Jehovah. The king then called priests to minister before the idols who were not from the tribe of Lehi, the priestly inheritance of Aaron. Thus, ten of the northern tribes broke away and became the Kingdom of Israel, headquartered in Samaria. The southern tribes of Judah and Benjamin allied themselves with Rehoboam and become known as the Kingdom of Judah, headquartered in Jerusalem.[8]

The wickedness continued in Israel despite the preaching of prophets such as Elijah, Elisha, Hosea, and Jonah.[9] Finally, the people had continued to pervert themselves before heathen gods and had become what a Book of Mormon scripture later referred to as *ripe with iniquity* (see 1 Nephi 17:35). Those who were righteous left Israel and fled south to the Kingdom of Judah. Judah was no paragon of virtue, but she did have good moments when there was a righteous king upon the throne. With very few righteous people left in Israel, God withdrew His hand of protection from them.

At that time, the Kingdom of Assyria was the major political and military power in the Middle East. In about 720 BC, the Assyrians conquered Samaria and deported most of the Israelites who survived the war. The Assyrians had a pattern of destruction that was so horrible that they are often called the first terrorists. They would spread the word before them of the terrible tortures awaiting those who resisted them until many cities just gave in immediately to escape the worst. They also had a practice of taking the people of one conquered nation and spreading them throughout their empire. They would then bring people from other parts of the empire to live in the conquered land. So profound was this disruption that the northern tribes disappeared as a cultural group, and to this day, no one knows for sure where they are; they are often called *the Lost Ten Tribes*. Some in Israel, seeing the coming disaster, fled to the south. A few inhabitants managed to stay under the radar and continue to live in the land, where they intermarried with people brought in from the east. These people came to be known as the Samaritans because the capital of the Northern Kingdom was Samaria. The bulk of the population was sent north and scattered so thoroughly that they completely disappeared as a people.

At the time of the Assyrian onslaught, Judah had a righteous king upon the throne. King Hezekiah listened to the prophet Isaiah. He knew what was coming. He called his people to repentance, cleansed the temple, and restored much of what was lost in Judah. He also prepared his city to withstand a prolonged siege. One of his most notable projects was the building of a tunnel under the city to the city's water source, which was outside the city wall. Through Hezekiah's Tunnel, residents of Jerusalem were able to have access to water no matter what was happening outside.

The siege finally came. Most of the towns and cities in Judah had fallen, but not Jerusalem with its temple. The Assyrian army was camped outside Jerusalem's gates waiting for morning to attack. Hezekiah and all the inhabitants in the city bowed down and prayed for deliverance. The King was reassured by the Lord through His prophet that He was in charge and that Jerusalem would not fall, nor would the temple.

That night, a mysterious event occurred. The scriptures tell us this:

> And it came to pass that night, that the angel of the Lord went out, and smote the camp of the Assyrians an hundred fourscore and five thousand [185,000]: and when they arose early in the morning, behold, they were all dead corpses. (2 Kings 19:35)[10]

Jerusalem was saved! Unfortunately, Hezekiah was followed to the throne by his unrighteous son, Manasseh, and the people again fell into wickedness. He was so wicked that he is often called Judah's equivalent to King Ahab of Israel. Tradition claims that it was Manasseh who ordered the death of Isaiah (see Appendix D, Old Testament Prophets).

About a hundred years after the fall of Israel, power in the Middle East shifted and the Kingdom of New Babylon took center stage. The Kingdom of Judah still existed, although things were politically tenuous. With Babylon to the east and Egypt to the south, the Jewish nation had to walk a fine line. Geographically speaking, the kingdom was right on the main trade route between Egypt in the south and the kingdoms of Mesopotamia in the northeast. There was a brief respite from wickedness with the reign of the righteous King Josiah. Josiah made one mistake and it cost him his life. Pharaoh Necho of Egypt asked Josiah if he could cross through Judah to Babylon. The prophets warned Josiah not to put himself between Egypt and Babylon, but he did. He sent out his armies against the pharaoh and was mortally wounded in that battle.

After his death, his son, Jehoahhaz, took the throne. He was a weak king and only ruled for three months. He was soon removed from the throne by Pharaoh Necho and replaced by his older brother, a puppet king, Eliakim, whom Necho renamed Jehoiakim. Jehoiakim held the throne for Judah as a vassal to Egypt. Jehoiakim reigned eleven years and was replaced by his son, Jeconiah, who ruled for only three months.

During the reign of Jehoiakim, Babylon defeated Egypt at the Battle of Carchemish, and the Kingdom of Judah became a vassal state, paying tribute to Babylon instead of Egypt. Many of its brightest and wisest were taken captive into Babylon to be educated in the ways of the Chaldeans.[11] Among these were Daniel and his three friends, who are best known by their Babylonian names, Shadrach, Meshach, and Abednego. A second deportation happened a few years later when others were taken, including a priest named Zachariah, who became God's prophet to the Jews in captivity in Babylon.

A puppet king, Zedekiah, was placed on the throne of Judah and required to pay an even larger tribute to Babylon. Zedekiah reigned for nine years and was such a wicked king that he led the people in gross wickedness. Again, the Lord sent prophets to warn the people, who had become as arrogant and prideful as their ruler. This was a difficult position for these prophets because the issues were political as well as religious. Religiously, the people claimed responsibility for their own blessings and forgot God. When prophets of God like Jeremiah warned them that Jerusalem would be destroyed unless the people repented, they scorned and ridiculed. "It can't happen to us," they said. "It can't happen here. The Assyrians didn't conquer us because we are God's people. No one will destroy God's city, Jerusalem. No one will destroy God's Temple."

The political side of the issue was that Zedekiah was leaning toward Egypt as an ally. Pharaoh had urged Judah to revolt, promising that Egypt would back them up. Of course, Pharaoh had no intention of helping Judah. He just wanted Judah to serve as a buffer between his kingdom and the Babylonians. It was a complex time both politically and religiously. When men like Lehi, Jeremiah, and other prophets spoke out against the wicked king and people, it was construed as treasonous. Other prophets whose names we may never know likely followed suit in the years between Manasseh and Zedekiah. Torture, imprisonment, and death were common sentences. That was what was facing Lehi and the other prophets.

It was at this point in history that the Book of Mormon began. It all started with the family of a prophet in Judah named Lehi.

Lehi: Prophet in Judah and in a New Land

Lehi, as mentioned, was a prophet to Judah and a contemporary of Jeremiah. He was warned by God in a vision to leave Jerusalem before the mobs could take his life. His son, Nephi, told the story:

> For it came to pass in the commencement of the first year of the reign of
> Zedekiah, king of Judah, . . . there came many prophets, prophesying
> unto the people that they must repent, or the great city Jerusalem must be
> destroyed.
>
> [M]y father, Lehi, . . . went forth to [pray] unto the Lord, yea, even with
> all his heart, in behalf of his people . . . as he prayed unto the Lord, there
> came a pillar of fire and dwelt upon a rock before him; and he saw and heard
> much; and because of the things which he saw and heard he did quake and
> tremble exceedingly. . . . He returned to his own house at Jerusalem; and he
> cast himself upon his bed, being overcome with the Spirit and the things
> which he had seen. And being thus overcome with the Spirit, he was carried
> away in a vision, even that saw the heavens open, and he thought he saw God
> sitting upon his throne. (1 Nephi 1:18, 20)

Lehi saw many other things in his vision and was given a book to read in
which he saw the fate of Jerusalem. He was moved by love for his people and,
taking little care for his own safety, took his testimony and his message to the
people. Nephi continued:

> My father, Lehi . . . went forth among the people, and began to prophesy
> and to declare unto them concerning the things which he had both seen and
> heard [concerning the destruction of Jerusalem.] And it came to pass that the
> Jews did mock him because of the things which he testified of them; for he
> truly testified of their wickedness and their abomination . . .
>
> And when the Jews heard these things they were angry with him; yea, even
> as with the prophets of old, whom they had cast out, and stoned, and slain;
> and they also sought his life that they might take it away. (1 Nephi 1:19–20)

Lehi continued to preach despite the threats to his life until one night
when he had a prophetic dream. In his dream, the Lord spoke to him and
said: "Blessed art thou Lehi, because of the things which thou have done; and
because thou has been faithful and declared unto this people the things which
I commanded thee, behold, they seek to take away thy life" (1 Nephi 2:1).

Lehi was thus warned by the Lord and commanded to take his family
into the wilderness. Lehi obeyed, I suspect with some haste, leaving behind
his house, his land of his inheritance, gold, silver, and other precious things.
He took only his family and the provisions and tents they would require for
survival.

I think it is interesting the way the Lord chose the missions of each of
these prophets. The Prophet Jeremiah was commanded to stay and continue
to preach, which he did. The Prophet Ezekiel was a priest of the tribe of Levi.
He was carried captive in the second raid on Judah. There in Babylon, God

called him to be a prophet to preach to the captives. Lehi was told to leave Judah and flee into the wilderness to escape Babylon. Unbeknownst to the Jews—and to Lehi himself at that time[12]—was the fact that Lehi was *not* a Jew, even though he lived in Judah. He was a descendant of *Joseph* through Joseph's son, Manasseh (not the same Manasseh who was a wicked king!). Lehi and his family were the fulfillment of Joseph's blessing, that he was to be a fruitful bough that would *run over the wall*. He and his family were led over the wall to a land that was "choice above all other lands" (1 Nephi 2:20). This is how that specific group of Israelites fit into the promised blessings of Israel, for a purpose only God knew at the time.

The Sons of Lehi

Lehi had four sons during the time he lived near Jerusalem: Laman, Lemuel, Sam, and Nephi. From the writings of Nephi, we learn that Lehi was a man of substance. Unfortunately, his two eldest sons never accepted their father as a prophet. They thought him to be a visionary old man and resented having to leave their lands and wealth behind to live in tents in the Arabian Desert. Nephi, the youngest, was a righteous young man who believed his father and later became a prophet himself. Sam, the third son, aligned himself with Nephi.

A Geographical Perspective

So far, I have placed the story of Israel in time. I will now look at placing it in space: a geographical perspective on these ancient scriptures. The story of Lehi's family began in the Kingdom of Judah. It is important to note that Nephi speaks of his father living *at* Jerusalem, not *in* Jerusalem (1 Nephi 1:4). He also speaks of the *land* of Jerusalem rather than just the city of Jerusalem. In the same way, the Northern Kingdom of Israel was often referred to as Samaria because that was the name of its capital city, but not everything in the *land* of Samaria was within the city of Samaria.

When Lehi's family left the land of Jerusalem, which way did they go? While I have seen no maps of a prophetically identified route,[13] the Book of Mormon itself provides many clues as to the direction of Lehi's journey. Pragmatically, he could not have gone north without running right into Assyria, which, while not the power that it had been, was still a dangerous foe. To have gone east would have meant walking right into the Babylonians. West would have meant the ocean. At that point in time, we don't know what Lehi's profession was, but we do know that he lived in a desert. It is obvious that he wasn't a seafarer. Going south for any distance would have put the family in danger in

Egypt. There was little choice but to go southeast, and then across the Arabian Peninsula, keeping away from other caravans and people as much as possible.

In 1950, Dr. Hugh Nibley published a series of articles in the Church magazine *The Improvement Era* that was called "Lehi in the Desert."[14] Taking this as a starting point, Latter-day Saints Lynn and Hope Hilton undertook a massive project: traveling what they believe was Lehi's trail, using only the Book of Mormon as their guide for distances and directions. Their findings were published in the *Ensign* and *Liahona* magazines in September and October of 1976. Many of the ideas shared here have come from their research.

The Book of Mormon states that Lehi and his family left the land of Jerusalem with haste and traveled down near the border of the Red Sea. From there, they likely followed what was by then an already ancient trading route called the Frankincense Trail. They would have needed to follow the available wells of the spice merchants, at the same time avoiding larger settlements.

1 Nephi 2:6 reports that Lehi traveled three days into the wilderness. Some readers of the Book of Mormon have construed this to mean three days from Jerusalem. A look at a map of the area would indicate that it is much farther than a three-day journey from Jerusalem to the Red Sea. A careful reading of 1 Nephi 2:5–6 shows that it was *after* the family had arrived at the borders of the Red Sea that they turned east and traveled three days into the wilderness before pitching their tents and making a semi-permanent camp in a valley Lehi called Lemuel near a river that he named Laman.

They hadn't been there long when Lehi received another vision in which the Lord commanded him to send his sons back to the land of Jerusalem to obtain a certain record in the possession of a distant cousin, an unrighteous man named Laban. While I won't go into the details of their journey or the problems they encountered in obtaining the record, the fact that they got it was crucial to them and to us. This record contained the genealogy of Lehi's family, and it also contained the five books of Moses and the writings of several of the prophets, including Isaiah. Because of this record, Lehi found out that he was a Josephite and not a Jew. The record helped them preserve their language, their culture, and their religion. They quite literally would have been lost without it, as would we have been lost had it not been preserved, in part, on the pages of the record they left behind that we know as the Book of Mormon.

Lehi's sons were sent back to the land of Jerusalem a second time to convince another cousin, this time a righteous man named Ishmael, to bring his family and join Lehi in the wilderness. Ishmael was also a descendant of Joseph, this time through Ephraim, making the circle of Joseph's promise complete.

Eventually, they settled in a place that they called Bountiful because it was green and fertile. The Hiltons hypothesized that it may have been in the area known today as the Sultanate of Oman,[15] which is very green and beautiful. Laman and Lemuel wanted to stay there, but Lehi told them that this was not *the land choice above all other lands* (1 Nephi 13:30) promised by God.

After much prayer, hard work, and adversity, Nephi succeeded in building a boat. Trusting their care to the Lord, they set sail and eventually landed in America. No one knows for sure where the site of first landing was, but many LDS scholars believe it was in what is now southern Guatemala.[16]

During their years in the desert, Lehi had two more sons. He named them Jacob and Joseph after his forefathers in Genesis 39 to 50. When Lehi died in the new land, the older brothers, Laman and Lemuel, sought to kill Nephi, along with Jacob, Joseph, and Sam, who all followed Nephi. The two groups became known, respectively, as the Lamanites and the Nephites, living in the land where the Lord led them.

When I first read the Book of Mormon in my teens, I used to think that the story took place in all North and South America. I think a lot of Latter-day Saints thought that at one time or another. But in-depth scientific research studies, primarily conducted by LDS anthropologists, archeologists, and other scholars, have concluded that the Book of Mormon took place in an area ranging from Central Mexico to Guatemala and Belize.[17] While the blessings of the "land choice above all other lands" include both continents, the land occupied during Book of Mormon times by Book of Mormon people was much more limited.[18]

Scholars have been able to judge relative distances based on descriptions within the book itself of travel between cities by armies, travelers, and explorers. They also find clues in descriptions of the topography (mountains, valleys, rivers, and so on). Book of Mormon scholars believe they can quite accurately pinpoint about 80 percent of the sites mentioned in the book.[19]

Other People Who Were There

Another mistake many Latter-day Saints make is assuming that the people described in the Book of Mormon were the only people living in all North and South America. This is not true. There were many other groups of people indigenous to the area before Lehi's family ever arrived. There are indications within the book that Laman's and Lemuel's families intermarried with some of these people, which could explain the changes in their appearance noted in 2 Nephi 5:21. It could also explain why the Lamanites outnumbered the Nephites within the space of a generation or two. Where did these other people come from? No one knows for sure. I was always taught in school that some of them migrated from Asia, across the Bering Strait, following the herds. I understand that today, most Native American groups find that theory unacceptable because those theories do not fit well with their own traditions. The point of my discussion here is not *where* they came from but the fact that they were *here*. The Book of Mormon is *not* the story of the entire hemisphere, but of a small geographical area and of, essentially, one family.

Climate Changing Records: Nephi's Challenge

The Lord has always commanded His people to be a record-keeping people. Ancient prophets wrote on papyrus, parchment scrolls, and clay tablets. Even a thin metal scroll was found among the Dead Sea Scrolls. Early Christians prized the letters they received from Apostles such as John, Peter, and Paul. It is because they prized these words, copied them down, and saved them that we have the Old and the New Testaments today. The dry climate in the Middle East helped preserve documents and artifacts of earlier inhabitants of the area.

The people of the Book of Mormon were also commanded to keep records. In fact, Nephi was specifically commanded to keep a record of his people on thin sheets of gold (see 1 Nephi 9). Nephi may have wondered why God was so specific that the records be preserved in this way because it is much more difficult to engrave on metal than it is to write on parchment or clay. Nevertheless, he did as he was commanded. Had he not done so, we would not have the Book of Mormon today. The heat and humidity of the new land would have destroyed parchment and clay within a few short years at best. Only metal— and in this case gold, which does not rust—could have survived millennia.

Day-to-day records were probably kept on parchment or clay tablets, but the important things would have been preserved in gold. The ninth chapter of 1 Nephi also tells us that Nephi kept more than one set of plates. The Nephites also had in their possession the Plates of Laban, which were made of brass. They would eventually have access to the metal plates that contained the records of the Jaredites, a group who left the Middle East after the fall of the Tower of Babel.[20]

Fate of Israel: The Parable of the Olive Tree

Before I leave the theme of the house of Israel, I think it is important to look at the parable of the olive tree. The scriptures are replete with examples of the house of Israel, God's people, depicted as a vineyard or an orchard, usually of olive trees. Olive trees are indigenous to the Middle East and highly prized.

The way olive trees are cultivated and tended to make them the perfect metaphor for God's dealing with the house of Israel. The primary message of the olive tree metaphor is that, though God may scatter Israel because of their sins, He will gather them in at the end.

Paul makes a reference to the parable in his letter to the Romans, chapter 11. Paul was the Apostle called to take the gospel to the Gentiles. In this chapter of Romans, Paul is attempting to explain the role of the Gentiles in the kingdom of God by likening it to the branches of a wild olive tree (the Gentiles) being grafted into the tame olive tree (the house of Israel) and of dead branches of the original tree (Israelites lost to apostasy) being cut away. It almost seems as if Paul was paraphrasing from an original source to which we have no access in our current Bible.

We have a much more detailed account of the parable in the book of Jacob, chapter 5, in the Book of Mormon. Jacob is quoting a prophecy from the Plates of Brass Nephi obtained from Laban. It is from the writings of a prophet named Zenos, who must have prophesied to the Israelites at some time prior to Lehi's life—a prophet of whom we have no record in our current Old Testament or Hebrew Bible. I won't take the time to quote the entire parable, for it is lengthy, only to say that the way Zenos describes the culture and care of olive trees is consistent with the way these trees have been raised for millennia. It is very different from other fruit trees to the degree that no one in nineteenth-century America could have known anything about olive farming even approaching what is described by Jacob. Jacob himself was quoting from a different source (Zenos) because he had been born in the wilderness and had likely never seen an olive tree himself.

Paul's reference is spotty. Jacob's reference is exact. This parable shows the entire fate of the house of Israel from its beginnings and is just one example of how the Book of Mormon, in this case, amplifies and clarifies a Biblical reference.

Notes

1. Ezra Taft Benson, "The Book of Mormon Is the Word of God," *Ensign*, May 1975.
2. See Appendix A for a clarification of the various names of God, referencing the Father, the Son, and the Holy Ghost.
3. *Joseph and the Amazing Technicolor Dreamcoat*, Andrew Lloyd Webber, 1968–1982 from first draft to Broadway.
4. Ishmael was the eldest son of Abraham, son of Sarah's handmaiden Hagar.
5. The geographical area in Egypt where the Children of Israel lived.

6. Whenever you see the word *LORD* all in caps in the Old Testament, it is referring to Jehovah or Yahweh, the Great I AM.

7. See 2 Samuel 12:1–12 for Nathan's brilliant parable that exposed David's sin.

8. The full events of these kingdoms can be found in the Biblical books of First and Second Kings and First and Second Chronicles. To see maps of the Twelve Tribes under the Judges, the Kingdoms of David and Solomon, and the division into two separate kingdoms, see the maps section of the LDS Scriptures or go to www.lds.org maps.

9. Jonah is best known for running away from God and being swallowed by a big fish. Later he preached in Nineveh, but he also preached to the people in Israel.

10. The prophet Isaiah also wrote of this experience in Isaiah 37:36.

11. The Chaldeans were the people who inhabited the area of Mesopotamia and included the Assyrians and the Babylonians.

12. Lehi didn't know his genealogy until Nephi secured brass plates from a distant cousin, Laban (1 Nephi 5:14–16).

13. The Church of Jesus Christ of Latter-day Saints has never made any official statement as to where Lehi and his family traveled or where they arrived when they reached the Promised Land. Any points that I make, therefore, should not be construed to be an official reflection of the Church's position on this issue. Rather, my ideas are based on the writing of LDS scholars, explorers, and archeologists.

14. Lynn N. Hilton and Hope A. Hilton, "In Search of Lehi's Trail," *Ensign*, September 1976.

15. Ibid.

16. John L. Sorenson, *An Ancient American Setting for the Book of Mormon* (Salt Lake City: Deseret Book and Provo, UT: The Foundation for Ancient Research and Mormon Studies, 1996).

17. Ibid.

18. There is some disagreement among scholars as to the possible location of Lehi's colony. I have heard hypotheses ranging from Baja California to the Mound Builders of the eastern United States. I personally have no argument with any of these people and I am not an archaeologist. I am using the Central America hypothesis presented by Sorenson and others simply for convenience in looking at a broad picture. What happened is far more important than where it happened. As mentioned earlier, the Church has never made a definitive statement as the location of Book of Mormon lands.

19. Sorensen, *An Ancient American Setting for the Book of Mormon*.

20. For an account of the Jaredites, see the book of Ether in the Book of Mormon.

THEME 2

Covenants and Ordinances

This theme involves the relationship of the house of Israel with the making and keeping of sacred covenants. What is a covenant? Why are Israel's covenant relationships important to us today? What happens when one of the parties violates a covenant? How does the Book of Mormon reflect and clarify covenants discussed in the Bible? How do ordinances relate to covenants?

Nephi made plates of gold upon which to write in about 570 BC, thirty years after he and his family left Jerusalem. It is around this time that his father, Lehi, died, leaving Nephi in charge of the spiritual care of the family. Laman and Lemuel and the sons of Ishmael rebelled against Nephi, causing him and his family, along with Sam, Jacob, and Joseph, to leave their homes and move into the mountains, away from their hostile brethren. There, they built a temple.

About 559 to 545 BC, Nephi called his people together to a meeting for sacred instruction. He asked his younger brother Jacob (who by then, of course, was a man) to speak to the people about their heritage as part of the house of Israel (see 2 Nephi 6). He was concerned that they seemed to have lost sight of that. He quoted from the writings of Isaiah, which the Nephites had on the Plates of Brass, and then he made it personal by reminding them that they were a covenant people.

> And now, my beloved brethren, I have read these things that ye might know concerning the covenants of the Lord that he has *covenanted* with all the house of Israel—
>
> That he has spoken unto the Jews, by the mouth of his holy prophets, even from the beginning down, from generation to generation, until the time comes that they shall be restored to the true church and fold of God . . .
>
> Behold, my beloved brethren, I speak unto you things that ye may rejoice and lift up your heads forever, because of the blessings which the Lord God shall bestow upon your children. (2 Nephi 9:1–3; emphasis added)

What Is a Covenant?

In this context, a covenant is a promise between God and man. It is most sacred. Covenants are two-way promises. God promises great blessings for His part, but in return, He expects us to keep our part of the promise. The Bible records many such covenants, as does the Book of Mormon. As Jacob said, God has been making covenants with His people from the beginning. The key covenants recorded in the Book of Mormon are related to the covenants God made with His people in Old Testament times. Understanding Biblical covenants helps us understand Book of Mormon covenants and place the Book of Mormon in the larger context of holy writ.

Adam and Eve

The Covenant to Multiply and Replenish; Agency and Procreation

While the Book of Genesis doesn't use the word *covenant* when speaking of Adam and Eve, there is an implicit covenant at work. The first commandment given in the Garden was to "multiply and replenish the earth" (Genesis 1:28).

God knew that it was not good for man to be alone, so he created Eve to be a *help meet*[1] for him (Genesis 2:20). To make procreation possible, God gave Eve to Adam to be his wife (Genesis 2:24).

After God created Adam, he gave him a commandment that he could eat of any tree in the garden except the tree of the knowledge of good and evil. If he did so, he would become mortal and subject to death (Genesis 2:17). We now understand that this was part of Heavenly Father's plan. Without becoming mortal, Adam and Eve could not have kept God's first commandment that they multiply and replenish the earth. I believe Eve understood this when she made the difficult decision to transgress one law to be physically able to keep the more important law. Adam, too, understood and partook. You might ask why God would place Adam and Eve in such a difficult position. The answer lies in the fact that human beings have agency. Mortality is such a challenging and often painful experience that God could not just thrust it upon them. They had to have the opportunity to make that choice themselves. I feel great gratitude toward our first parents because without their courageous choice, God's plan for His children would have been thwarted and we would not exist.

After partaking of the forbidden fruit, Adam and Eve became mortal. They understood the difference between good and evil. Prior to the Fall, they could not have entered a covenant with God because they were as innocent as a newborn child. But after the Fall, they were able to be held accountable, knowing good from evil, and were thus capable of making covenants with God.

21

God's part of the covenant as recorded in the third chapter of Genesis sounds more like a punishment than a covenant, and most of the world interprets it as such. But a prayerful reading of the text clearly points to promises and even blessings. To Eve, He promises conception and childbirth. The world sees the word *sorrow* and thinks *curse*. But God is giving Eve a tremendous gift—the ability to become a co-creator with Him in providing mortal bodies for His spiritual children. God gave to Eve the promise of motherhood.

To Adam, God promised toil—weeds instead of fruit. But the key word that this is a blessing and not a cursing is found in these words of verse 17: "for thy sake." Work is a blessing. Caring for and protecting a wife and children is a blessing. Accomplishing a job well done is a blessing. Adam and Eve were blessed rather than cursed and, even though times were difficult, they came to understand the blessings they had been given and they worshipped God in gratitude and joy (Moses 5:10–11).

The Book of Mormon prophet Jacob dealt with the topic of the divine nature of marriage as a God-ordained covenant and the importance of marital fidelity. In his sermon, he dealt with a problem that plagued the Nephites, men justifying infidelity through multiple wives and concubines (Jacob 2). To these men, Jacob wrote:

> Ye have broken the hearts of your tender wives, and lost the confidence of your children, because of your bad examples before them; and the sobbing's of their hearts ascend up to God against you . . . many hearts died, pierced with deep wounds. (Jacob 2:35)

Marriage is a three-way covenant between a man and a woman and God. That covenant God made with our first parents still stands today. In a sacred and sober proclamation, "The Family: A Proclamation to the World," the First Presidency of The Church of Jesus Christ of Latter-day Saints and the Quorum of the Twelve Apostles made the following statement, which I quote only in part:

> The first commandment that God gave to Adam and Eve pertained to their potential for parenthood as husband and wife. We declare that God's commandment for His children to multiply and replenish the earth remains in force. We further declare that God has commanded that the sacred powers of procreation are to be employed only between man and woman, lawfully wedded as husband and wife. . . .
>
> We declare the means by which mortal life is created is divinely appointed. We affirm the sanctity of life and of its importance in God's eternal plan.[2]
>
> The family is ordained of God. Marriage between man and woman is essential to His eternal plan. Children are entitled to birth within the bonds

22

of matrimony, and to be reared by a father and a mother who honor marital vows with complete fidelity.

Many today choose to ignore this admonition. The family proclamation reminds us that they do so to their own sorrow.[3]

The Covenant Law of Sacrifice

The second covenant that God made with Adam and Eve was the law of sacrifice. Adam's part of the covenant was to sacrifice the firstling of his flocks, a male lamb without blemish, upon the altar. This was an economic sacrifice for Adam and Eve, who relied on their flocks for nourishment and clothing. God's part of the covenant was that He would provide the ultimate sacrifice, the gift of His Only Begotten, to save us from sin and death. The sacrifice of a firstborn and perfect lamb, therefore, represented the ultimate sacrifice of Jesus Christ, the Lamb of God.

We know that they kept this law and taught it to their children because their son, Abel, kept that law as recorded in Genesis 4. That God was specific as to the terms of the covenant is shown in the fact that He "respected" Abel and his offering of a lamb but did not respect Cain and his offering of grain. It wasn't that Cain didn't have a lamb; it was that Cain tried to change the ordinance as it had been given by God, which was a violation of the covenant. It is implicit that Cain had also willingly covenanted with Satan (see Moses 5:29). God knew that Cain's intent was not honest. He knew Cain's heart.

This covenant to offer sacrifice by the shedding of blood was fulfilled in the sacrifice of the Only Begotten Son of the Father, Jesus Christ. Today, we offer the sacrifice of a broken heart and a contrite spirit as we take part in the ordinance of the sacrament each week. Adam sacrificed to look forward to Christ. We sacrifice as we partake of the sacrament in remembrance of Christ. The Book of Mormon records the words of a king who said: "God . . . I will give away all my sins to know thee" (Alma 22:18). That is our sacrifice—to give away all our sins.

Noah and the Rainbow

Differentiating between Covenants and the Tokens That Represent Them

God's covenants with Noah are recorded in Genesis 6–9. The first covenant was that if Noah would build the ark as God specified and gather the animals according to God's prospectus, God would see to it that Noah, his wife, his three sons, and their wives would be kept safe within the ark and not be destroyed in the flood.

God's second covenant with Noah is recorded in Genesis 9 and is the beautiful promise that God will never destroy the entire earth by flood again. The token of that covenant is a rainbow.

It is important to understand that a token is something that is given as a reminder of a covenant. While it is not the covenant itself, it does bring the covenant to mind. The Bible dictionary states that the rainbow is "an outward token of God's covenant with Noah. . . . The rainbow no doubt existed before the Flood, but with Noah the rainbow took on a new significance as the token of the covenant."[4]

Noah's part of the covenant after the flood was to continue living the law of sacrifice as given to Adam. The first thing Noah did when leaving the ark was to build an altar and offer sacrifice to the Lord. Noah and his sons Ham, Shem, and Japheth, and their wives, were also commanded to fulfill the covenant to "multiply and replenish the earth" as had their first parents (Genesis 8, 9:1).

Abraham and His World-Blessing Covenant with God

Three Promises of the Abrahamic Covenant

Abraham also kept the ancient law of sacrifice. We know that he did because we first read about Abram (for so was he known at that time) in Genesis 12:1, and by Genesis 12:7, we learn that Abram built an altar to God.

Abram also covenanted with God, one of the most profound promises God ever gave to man. In the Church, we refer to this as the *Abrahamic Covenant*. Once we learn about this covenant, it becomes evident over and over in the lives of Abraham's descendants. One of the tokens of this covenant was that Abram's name was changed to *Abraham* and his wife's name was changed from Sarai to *Sarah*.

The Abrahamic covenant contains three key promises from the Lord:

- A promise of land
- A promise of posterity
- A promise that Abraham and his descendants would be God's people and would, therefore, be able to perform ordinances in His name, through God's priesthood

Abraham's part of the covenant was brief:

24

- He was to continue to keep the law of sacrifice.
- He was to worship only one God.
- He would continue to circumcise all male children by the age of eight days.

In this case, circumcision was the token of the covenant. It clearly set Abraham's descendants apart from the rest of the world, a mark, if you will, of a covenant people. This law and token were to be maintained by Abraham and his descendants until the Messiah came to fulfill the law through His Atonement and crucifixion, the ultimate sacrifice. Orthodox Jews and Muslims still practice circumcision to this day because, while many of them accept Jesus as a prophet, they do not accept him as the Son of God, the Messiah.

The Binding of Isaac, the Covenant, and Jesus Christ

Some years ago, I had an interesting experience watching a series on public television about the Book of Genesis.[5] The episode was about Abraham and the binding of Isaac found in Genesis 22. The panel discussing the story was made up of religious educators and clergy from several different faiths. Represented were a small group of Catholics, Protestants, Jews, and a Muslim.[6] Other than the Muslim, whose response was *in sha Allah,*[7] the other members of the group were appalled at the passage! Several said that God would never ask a man to sacrifice his child. Others said Abraham was old and senile and probably imagined that he'd been commanded. One even suggested that Abraham was schizophrenic! I was stunned! I couldn't believe that none of them, particularly the Christian scholars, saw no connection between what Abraham was being asked to do and what God would one day do: offer His Only Begotten Son as a propitiation for sin.

A few days later, as I was studying Jacob in the *Book of Mormon,* I read:

> Behold, they [our first parents] believed in Christ and worshiped the Father in his name, and, we worship the Father in his name. And for this intent we keep the law of Moses, it pointing our souls to him; and for this cause it is sanctified unto us for righteousness, *even as it was accounted unto Abraham in the wilderness to be obedient unto the commands of God in offering up his son Isaac, which is a similitude of God and his Only Begotten Son.* (Jacob 4:5; emphasis added)

No wonder those other religious scholars were confused! The binding of Isaac can be a disturbing story unless one understands that the call to sacrifice Isaac was a foreshadowing of the sacrifice of Jesus Christ. Abraham, as the father of the covenant, had to understand at an emotionally deep level the sacrifice of the Father in giving His Only Begotten Son. God gave the commandment knowing full well that Abraham would never actually be required to carry it out. Only through the Book of Mormon does the proposed sacrifice of Isaac make any sense.

It was important for Isaac, too. He wasn't a small child but a young man. Through this experience, Isaac came to understand the willingness of the Son to sacrifice His own life for all.

In the end, Isaac's life was spared. Abraham learned that *God will provide himself a lamb* (Genesis 22:8). He did. That lamb is Jesus Christ, the Lamb of God.

Isaac took part in the renewal of God's covenant with his father, Abraham, when he was willing to give his life in obedience to God. So important was the covenant with God that when Isaac was of sufficient age to take a wife, Abraham sent a trusted servant to the home of a cousin to find a wife *of the covenant* for his son. He did not want Isaac to marry outside the covenant of the Lord. The story of how the servant found Rebecca, the one the Lord had chosen for Isaac, is found in Genesis 24:60. The Lord further renewed His covenant specifically with Isaac, as is recorded in Genesis 17:19.

Jacob, the Second Twin

Jacob was one of the twin sons born to Isaac and Rebecca. His father, Isaac, blessed him with the blessings of the covenant of Abraham. Like Abraham, Jacob's parents did not want him to marry outside the covenant as his brother Esau had. They sent him to Padan-aram to the home of his maternal grandfather to find a worthy bride.

One night during his travel, as he was sleeping on the top of a mountain, he dreamed of a ladder between heaven and earth. Angels were ascending and descending. The important thing about this vision in the context of covenants is that God renewed the covenant He made with Abraham and Isaac that night with Jacob on the mountaintop: land, posterity, and being God's chosen people. Jacob later married, and he fathered twelve sons, including Joseph, as I discussed earlier. The Abrahamic Covenant was passed on through Jacob to his sons. Like Abraham, Jacob was also given a new name as a token of his entering into the covenant: *Israel*.

God's chosen people were promised a specific land, described in Exodus as a "land flowing with milk and honey" (Exodus 3:8). They would have peace and prosperity in the land. They could grow mighty in the land through their posterity. They would be God's people and He would be their God. All these promised blessings were made on the condition of Israel's obedience.

Covenants in the Book of Mormon

The Book of Mormon is intimately connected with the Bible. The Old Testament covenants given to Adam, Noah, and Abraham are carried out in the Book of Mormon. Lehi was a descendant of Abraham through Isaac, Jacob (Israel), and Joseph. It is not surprising that he and his descendants were heirs to Abraham's covenant.

Before Lehi died, he blessed his sons, as had Israel. He named his youngest son Joseph after the very Joseph who was sold into Egypt. Lehi addressed Joseph as he began his blessing:

> For behold, thou are the fruit of my loins; and I am a descendant of Joseph who was carried captive into Egypt. And great were the covenants of the Lord which he made unto Joseph. (2 Nephi 3:4)

I don't recall reading anywhere in the Old or New Testament a specific reference to God's renewing the Abrahamic Covenant with Joseph, as he had with Isaac and Jacob, but it seems clear to me from this verse in the Book of Mormon that He did.

A query of the scriptures on LDS.org indicates that the word *covenant* appears 256 times in the Old Testament, 23 times in the New Testament, and 131 times in the Book of Mormon. Many of those Book of Mormon references are to the Abrahamic Covenant as it applies to the descendants of Joseph.

A Land Choice above All Other Lands

Upon landing in their new home, Lehi spoke to his family. He reminded them how merciful the Lord had been in warning them to flee out of the land of Jerusalem, because he had seen in a vision that, since they left and while they were in the wilderness, Jerusalem had indeed been destroyed, and had they stayed, they would have been destroyed as well. He then went on to say the following:

> But, said he, notwithstanding our afflictions, we have obtained a land of promise, a land which is choice above all other lands, a land which the Lord God have covenanted with me should be a land for the inheritance of my seed. Yea, the Lord hath covenanted this land unto me, and to my children forever, and also all those who should be led out of other countries by the hand of the Lord. (1 Nephi: 3–5)

Thus, it appears that God renewed the covenant of a Promised Land with Lehi for his descendants. However, the descendants have a part in this covenant, that they should serve God and keep his commandments. Insofar as they would do that, this would be a land of liberty and they would never be brought into captivity as had happened in both Israel and Judah. However, if they allowed themselves to forget their God, they would have no promise. Only iniquity would lead them to be cursed in the land (2 Nephi 2:7). This promise is repeated over and over in the Book of Mormon. It is amazing to me how many times the people forgot it.

The Promise of Posterity

While I don't know that there is any count of the numbers of descendants Lehi had, we can safely assume it was numbered in the hundreds of thousands, if not millions. By the time the people had destroyed themselves as a people (around AD 400), the Book of Mormon numbers the casualties in the tens of thousands. The Lord promised Abraham that all the world would be blessed through his posterity. The same can be said for Lehi, whose descendants live on today.

King Mosiah, a righteous king in the Book of Mormon, said this about his posterity:

> And now I desire that this inequality should be no more in this land, especially among this my people; but I desire that this land be a land of liberty and every man may enjoy his rights and privileges alike, so long as the Lord sees fit that we may live and inherit the land, yea, even as long as any of our posterity remains upon the face of the land. (Mosiah 29:32)

Lehi's Posterity: God's People and the Priesthood

I will talk more about the priesthood in Theme 3, discussing the topic from both volumes of ancient scripture. Suffice it to say that Lehi and his righteous descendants had the same priesthood as the ancient Biblical patriarchs. If the people remembered God and worshiped Him only, they were blessed with the blessings of the covenant. When they fell away, they had no such blessings. We are given that same blessing today. The Lord told the Prophet Joseph Smith: "I, the Lord, am bound when ye do what I say; but when ye do not what I say, ye have no promise" (D&C 82:10).

One of the key covenantal themes of the Book of Mormon relates to the promise of land. Abraham's descendants were given lands of promise according to their faithfulness. For Lehi and his family, that land was here in the Americas. While we may not know exactly where, we do know that this promise extends to all the land, including that nation we know as the United States.

28

This promise of a land, choice above all other lands, is mentioned fourteen times in the Book of Mormon, in the writings of Nephi and Jacob and an even more ancient prophet named Ether. In every single instance, the promise is given with the caveat that God will faithfully keep His part of the covenant if the people will keep theirs, which is to worship the God of the land, even Jesus Christ. When the majority of the people fail to do so and fall away into sin, they have no promise. God withdraws his hand and the people are left with the consequences.

The Covenant and the Pride Cycle

Earlier, I discussed the fact that people of the Book of Mormon were told they would be led to a land *choice above all other lands*. Like many of God's promises, this is a covenant. In fact, it is part of the Abrahamic Covenant: land, posterity, and being God's people. Lehi, as a descendant of Abraham through Jacob and Joseph, was promised a specific land. Lehi and his family were to be God's people—to have His commandments and His priesthood. If they kept God's commandments and honored and worshipped Him as their God, they would prosper in the land, both they and their posterity. If they did not, then God would withdraw His protection and leave them to experience the consequences of their own choices. It isn't that God delighted in punishing them; He loved them and wanted to bless them. But through disobedience, they tied His hands. He cannot bless His children in their sins any more than any parent could reward a child for deliberate disobedience, lest the child think that wickedness brings happiness, and it does not. The Law of the Harvest says we reap what we sow.

In the Book of Mormon, this is often referred to as the pride cycle (see Appendix D: The Pride Cycle). When the people remember God and obey, they are blessed. As their blessings lead them to prosperity, they forget God. They become prideful and claim that their blessings are due solely to their own efforts. They begin to mistreat their less fortunate neighbors and set up a social class system. They begin to disobey.

As they become more disobedient and wicked, God withdraws His blessings and protection. They are left to experience the natural consequences of their own arrogant and wicked choices—consequences that are often very painful! If their suffering humbles them, they begin to repent. They call upon God and promise to obey. If they are sincere, and their actions show true repentance, God is then able to bless them again according to the covenant.

I will discuss the effects of the pride cycle of Israel in the Old Testament and the Book of Mormon in more detail in Theme 4.

Ordinances

On LDS.org, we read this definition of the word *ordinance*:

> In the Church, an ordinance is a sacred, formal act performed by the authority of the priesthood. Some ordinances are essential to our exaltation. These ordinances are called saving ordinances. They include baptism, confirmation, ordination to the Melchizedek Priesthood (for men), the temple endowment, and the marriage sealing. With each of these ordinances, we enter into solemn covenants with the Lord.[8]

I have heard it said that if the covenant is the contract, then the ordinance is our signature on the contract.[9] It signifies before the Lord and those who witness the ordinance (at least two witnesses are required) that we have accepted the terms of the covenant. Ordinances require specific authority from God to be recognized and accepted by Him. This point is made particularly clear in the New Testament. I will discuss this authority to act in God's name in Theme 3.

There were ordinances performed in the Old Testament, such as those performed under the law of sacrifice, which I will discuss later. For the purposes of this discussion, I will focus on those ordinances mentioned specifically in the New Testament and in the Book of Mormon. So as to make this study a little easier, I will present my findings in a table. The charts show the Biblical reference, a brief description of the event, and the principle thus demonstrated. While there are many examples of healings and miracles in the texts, I have chosen only those that clearly refer to the exercise of *specific priesthood authority* in performing ordinances—for example, "laid their hands" or "ordained." At the end of each section, I will give the Book of Mormon quotes on each topic to show how much clarity the Book of Mormon brings to the understanding of priesthood ordinances.

The Ordinances of Baptism and the Gift of the Holy Ghost

Acts 8:14–17	The Apostles at Jerusalem heard that new converts in Samaria hadn't received the Holy Ghost. They had been baptized by *Aaronic* Priesthood authority, but had not yet had the Holy Ghost conferred upon them. Therefore, Peter and John went to Samaria. They conferred the Holy Ghost upon the baptized people, by the laying on of hands, because they held *Melchizedek* priesthood authority. The Apostles accepted that the baptism of the people had been performed by someone with proper authority and did not have them rebaptized.

Acts 19:1–6	In contrast, when Paul went to Ephesus, he was greeted by a group of disciples who also had not yet received the Holy Ghost. Paul asked them "unto what were they baptized," and they told him "unto the baptism of John." Under those circumstances, Paul had them rebaptized, and then they received the Holy Ghost by the laying on of Paul's hands. Because they hadn't been baptized into Christ's Church and because Paul didn't know what authority, if any, the baptizer had,[10] Paul chose to have them rebaptized. He then laid hands upon them and performed the priesthood ordinance necessary for them to receive the Holy Ghost. Proper authority is necessary for the ordinances to be accepted by God. When authority is called into question, the ordinance is performed again.
Ephesians 4:5	Paul taught the Ephesians that there is "One Lord, one faith, one baptism." The mode of performing priesthood ordinances is specified by the Lord and men may not take it upon themselves to make changes.
1 Corinthians 15:29	The Corinthian saints were having a difficult time accepting the idea of a literal resurrection. In Paul's first epistle to Corinth, he spent a great deal of time teaching about the resurrection. In one verse, he used the example of baptism for the dead as a proof of the reality of the resurrection. This is the only mention of priesthood ordinances for the dead in the New Testament and it is presented in an "oh, by the way" manner such that most Christians find it difficult to explain. Modern revelation teaches us that baptism for the dead is a priesthood ordinance.
Book of Mormon: 2 Nephi 31:13	Wherefore, my beloved brethren, I know that if ye follow the Son, with full purpose of heart, acting no hypocrisy, and no deception before God, but with real intent, repenting of your sins, witnessing unto the Father that ye are willing to take upon you the name of Christ, by baptism—yea, by following your Lord and your Savior down into the water, according to his word, behold, then shall ye receive the Holy Ghost; yea, then cometh the baptism of fire and of the Holy Ghost; and then can ye speak with the tongue of angels and shout praise to the Holy One of Israel. This is a direct quote from the words of Nephi. This is another way the Book of Mormon clarifies and explains the process by which one approaches baptism (also see Alma 7:15).

Book of Mormon: Moroni 8:10	Behold, I say unto you that this thing shall ye teach—repentance and baptism unto those who are accountable and capable of committing sin. This is a direct quote from a letter written by Mormon to his son Moroni, stating that baptism is only for those who are capable of understanding the consequences of right and wrong. Latter-day revelation teaches that children are not cognitively capable of such understanding until they are eight years old.[11]

Book of Mormon: Moroni 8:10–16	It is a solemn mockery before God that ye should baptize little children.
	    Behold, I say unto you that this thing shall ye teach—repentance and baptism unto those who are accountable and capable of committing sin. Teach parents that they must repent and be baptized.
	    . . . and their little children need no repentance nor baptism. Behold, baptism is unto repentance to the fulfilling the commandments unto the remission of sins.
	    But little children are alive in Christ, even from the foundation of the world; if not so, God is a partial God, and also a changeable God, and [not] a respecter to persons; for how many little children have died without baptism?
	    Behold, if these children could not be saved without baptism, these must have gone to an endless hell.[12]
	    . . . he that supposeth that little children need baptism is in the gall of bitterness and the bond of iniquity. . . . For awful is the wickedness to suppose that God saveth one child because of baptism, and the other must perish because he hath no baptism.
	    Wo be unto them that shall pervert the ways of the Lord!
	
	This is a direct quote from Mormon's letter to Moroni regarding the practice of infant baptism. The Lord neither requires nor accepts infant baptism. This is just one of the ways the ordinance of baptism has been perverted by the philosophies of men and by a misunderstanding of the words of Jesus to Nicodemus about being born again by water and by spirit (John 3:3–5).

The Ordinance of Anointing and Administering to the Sick

Acts 9:1–18	Saul (later called Paul) had been persecuting the Christians. While he was on his way to Damascus, he had a vision of the Lord Jesus Christ. The experience left Saul so shaken that he was struck blind. For three days he did not eat or drink. There was in Damascus a man named Ananias who held the priesthood. The Lord called him to go to a certain house to heal Saul. Even though Ananias was afraid, he did as he was asked. Not just anyone could have healed Saul. It required one with proper priesthood authority—in this case, Ananias. The Lord was very specific with Ananias as to why he had to be the one, even though he was afraid of Saul.
James 5:14–15	The Apostle James taught, "Is there any sick among you? Let him call for the elders of the church; and let them pray over him, anointing him with oil in the name of the Lord." Healing and anointing the sick are Melchizedek priesthood ordinances, and elders hold the Melchizedek priesthood.

The Ordinance of the Sacrament of the Lord's Supper

Matthew 26:26–28; Mark 14:22–24; Luke 22:17–20	All the authors of the synoptic gospels are specific as to the manner of Jesus's institution of the sacrament. All say that He broke the bread and blessed it and blessed the cup before giving it to His Apostles. Jesus replaced the ordinance of sacrifice, which looked forward to His crucifixion, with the ordinance of the sacrament, which looks back in remembrance of His, the ultimate sacrifice.
Acts 2:42, 46; Acts 20:7–11	The disciples of Christ "broke bread" and partook of the sacrament often, most specifically on Sunday. The sacrament is an important priesthood ordinance that should be observed on a regular and frequent basis.
1 Corinthians 10:16–21; 11:19–29	Paul was very explicit with the Corinthian Christians as to the sacred nature of the ordinance of the sacrament. They had turned it into a meal, glutting themselves on the bread and even getting drunk on the wine! (verse 21). The most explicit explanation in the Bible of the sacrament and its importance in the Church of Jesus Christ is found in these chapters. I highly recommend that you read these references. The sacrament is sacred. We must partake worthily, reverently, and regularly.

Book of Mormon: Moroni 9:29, Moroni 4, 5	See that ye are not baptized unworthily; see that ye partake not of the sacrament of Christ unworthily; but see that ye do all things in worthiness, and do it in the name of Jesus Christ, the Son of the living God; and if ye do this, and endure to the end, ye will in nowise be cast out. In this quote from Mormon's letter to Moroni, we learn of the link between baptism and the sacrament. Modern revelation teaches us that to partake of the sacrament is to renew the same vows made at baptism. Mormon also stresses the necessity of personal honesty and worthiness in participating in both ordinances. Moroni gives the actual prayer to be said by the priest when administering the tokens of the sacrament.

When I talk about the Gathering of Israel in Theme 8, you will see that, as Israel is gathered to Christ and His Church, the final goal of the gathering is the temple—"the mountain of the Lord's house" (Isaiah 2:2). There they will make eternal covenants through temple ordinances. Most who have had a temple experience recall the sacred nature of those covenants and ordinances as the peak experience of their lives.

I will now look at the covenants and ordinances and the priesthood required to administer them.

Notes

1. Note: That does not say *helpmate*. It does not imply that she is in any way his inferior. The phrase *help meet*, in fact, states that she is his equal—unlike the other animals in the garden.
2. The rest of the world believes that sexual intercourse between Adam and Eve was the "original sin," and they use it as justification for infant baptism because children are born because of sexual intercourse between their parents. This is not true. Once they were mortal, Adam and Eve did conceive and bear children as they had covenanted to do. God wants this power of procreation to be exercised only within the bonds of a marriage of one man to one woman, but even when it is misused, any child born of that union is completely innocent and not tainted by sin.
3. See the final paragraph of the proclamation.
4. Bible Dictionary, "Rainbow."
5. Bill Maher, *Genesis: A Living Conversation.* PBS, 1996
6. Muslims, Jews, and Christians are all *people of the book,* and, therefore, descendants of Abraham.
7. *As Allah wills it* or *God willing;* the Muslim also believed the bound son was Ishmael, not Isaac.
8. "Ordinances," Gospel Topics, topics.lds.org.
9. BYU TV, *Discussions on the Old Testament,* www.BYUTV.org

10. John himself held the Aaronic Priesthood and had the authority to baptize. But John had many disciples who were not descendants of Aaron and did not hold the Aaronic Priesthood. The people in Ephesus were not baptized by John but by one of his disciples. Interestingly, there is a group of John's disciples called the Mandaeans, primarily in Iran, who practice immersion baptism to this day.

11. Note: Swiss psychologist Piagét determined that a child must move from what he called the Pre-operational Stage to the Concrete Operational Stage, which usually happens sometime about age seven or eight.

12. Some churches who continue to perform infant baptism have a saying: "Hell is crammed with infants damned." (From a private source of a member of one of those churches.)

THEME 3

The Priesthood: Authority to Act in God's Name

In the previous theme, I discussed covenants and the ordinances that seal the covenant. I have spoken about God's covenants with this people, particularly the Abrahamic Covenant, and why covenants and their accompanying ordinances are important, even today. But I cannot talk about covenants and ordinances without discussing the priesthood, the authority and power to act in God's name. What does the word *power* mean, in this context? How does it differ from temporal power? What power was upon the earth in the days of Adam, Noah, and Abraham? Who had authority to administer ordinances under the law of Moses? What happened to this authority after the death of Jesus's Apostles?

In describing God's power, one of my favorite Old Testament stories shows the literal power of God's priesthood: the story of Elijah and the priests of the pagan god, Ba'al.[1]

In the book of 1 Kings in the Old Testament, we learn that Elijah had been sent by God to call the people of Israel to repentance, along with their wicked rulers, King Ahab and Queen Jezebel. Elijah arranged to meet Ahab on the top of Mount Carmel in the northern Kingdom of Israel and asked Ahab to invite four hundred and fifty of the *prophets* (priests) of Ba'al, along with as many people of the kingdom as would come.

Ahab did so in hopes of capturing and killing Elijah. When everyone was assembled, Elijah turned to the people and said: "How long halt ye between two opinions? If the Lord be God, follow him: but if Ba'al, then follow him" (1 Kings 18:21). No one answered him.

Then Elijah proposed a contest to see whose god was most powerful. He instructed the prophets of Ba'al to bring two young bullocks. The bullocks were killed and prepared for sacrifice, and then one was placed upon dry wood on the altar of Ba'al. Elijah then asked the prophets of Ba'al to call upon their god to ignite the wood and their sacrifice.

36

The priests of Ba'al prayed to their god all morning, but nothing happened. Elijah asked them if Ba'al was away on a trip or, perhaps, sleeping. The priests of Ba'al cried out with more frenzy and cut themselves until their blood gushed out, but nothing happened.

When evening arrived, Elijah took twelve large stones, each representing one of the tribes of Israel, and repaired the altar of the Lord, which Ahab and Jezebel had destroyed years earlier. He dug a trench around the altar and laid wood on top of the stones. He placed the second bullock upon the wood. Elijah then instructed the people to bring four barrels of water to douse the sacrifice. They did so. He asked that they do it a second time and then a third. The water drenched the bullock, wood, and altar and filled the trench around it.

Then Elijah prayed that the Lord would ignite the sacrifice so that the people of Israel could see that the God of Israel was the only true God. Fire shot down from heaven. The heat was so intense that it "consumed the sacrifice, and the wood, and the stones, and the dust, and licked up the water that was in the trench" (1 Kings 18:38). The people of the Kingdom of Israel learned a valuable lesson that day—who was a god of hollow pomp and who was a God of Holy Power.

That power is the power of the priesthood. It gives authority, but it is also a very real power.

Priesthood

Priesthood is integral part of the third blessing of the covenant: to be God's people. In order for Israel to be God's people, they had to have someone who had specific authority from God to perform ordinances associated with covenants.

We sometimes have a problem with the word *power* because it so often connotes worldly power—power that is abused in human relationships, governments, and even churches. This is *not* the power of God of which we speak. The power that sent fire from heaven for Elijah is the same power by which "God created the heaven and the earth" (Genesis 1:1). It is the power of God's priesthood.

Throughout the history of the world, God has delegated His priesthood to mankind. This priesthood is the authority to act in God's name, to perform saving ordinances, and to bless the lives of God's children.

The Order of the Priesthood

The Patriarchal Order of the Priesthood—Adam to Abraham[2]

As we learn from Alma, the priesthood has been on the Earth since the days of Adam. Adam received his priesthood directly from God. From then on, the posterity of Adam received the priesthood from worthy father to worthy son. When the father was not worthy, the righteous man received his priesthood from another worthy priesthood holder; as we discussed earlier, this was the case with Abraham.

Abraham followed the patriarchal order of the priesthood, conferring authority on his sons, including Isaac, who then conferred the priesthood upon his son Jacob, also known as Israel.[3] During the years of enslavement in Egypt, we don't know exactly when and what happened to priesthood authority among the Israelites. I am confident that it was lost to apostasy brought on by slavery; however, the priesthood still existed among others of Abraham's descendants. Modern revelation tells us that Moses received his priesthood authority through his father-in-law, Jethro (D&C 84:6), who was a priest of Midian (Exodus 3:1) and a descendant of Abraham's son Midian with his wife Keturah (Genesis 25:1–2; 1 Chronicles 1:32). From modern revelation, we learn that in Adam's, Enoch's, and Noah's day, it was called the Holy Priesthood after the Order of the Son of God (D&C 107).

Melchizedek and the Order of the Higher Priesthood

Since the days of Abraham, this authority has been called the Melchizedek Priesthood. Those who hold this priesthood today have the same authority as the ancient patriarch. They administer the temporal covenants, such as baptism, as well as the higher ordinances, such as giving the gift of the Holy Ghost (confirmation after baptism), blessing the sick, conferring the priesthood on others when so directed, and other higher ordinances as required. Anciently, they could offer sacrifices to the Lord.

Modern revelation teaches us that "before the days of Melchizedek, the priesthood was called the Holy Priesthood, after the Order of the Son of God. But out of respect or reverence to the name of the Supreme Being, to avoid the too frequent repetition of his name, they, the Church, in ancient days, called that priesthood after Melchizedek, or the Melchizedek Priesthood (D&C 107:3, 4).

Why was it named after a man so briefly mentioned in scripture? It was "because Melchizedek was such a great high priest" (D&C 107:2).

In the beginning, the priesthood was given following a patriarchal order from father to son, beginning with Adam. In some instances, where a father was unworthy to hold the priesthood, priesthood authority could be conferred by another. Abraham received his priesthood from Melchizedek, King of Salem (D&C 84:14).

Although Melchizedek is a somewhat enigmatic figure in the Bible, his role relating to the priesthood should not be underestimated. Paul tells us that Jesus Christ Himself was "called of God a high priest after the order of Melchizedek" (Hebrews 5:10). Abraham recognized Melchizedek as the presiding high priest of the Lord and paid tithes to him (Genesis 14: 18–20).

The Book of Mormon provides vital information about Melchizedek not found in the Bible. Without these insights, we would be at a loss to understand this authority to act in God's name.

Much of the world today is confused by the entire concept of priesthood. The Catholic and Eastern Orthodox churches claim to have the priesthood, handed down from Peter. While many Protestant churches have ordained priests, they don't claim to have Peter's authority. Other Christian churches claim no authority by stating that there is no need for authority. This led to the justification by faith and the concept of "the priesthood of the believers."[4] As a result of this confusion, there is a great discrepancy among the Christian churches today relating to the priesthood, covenants, and ordinances. The Book of Mormon, together with modern-day revelation, clears the muddied waters of centuries and leaves a crystal-clear view of God's authority given to man.

The most concise description of the priesthood, its history, and its necessity is found in the Book of Mormon, specifically in Alma 13. Though the New Testament speaks of Jesus Christ as being a high priest after the order of Melchizedek (Hebrews 5:6), it doesn't give any details about this higher priesthood. The Book of Mormon provides answers to questions that are found nowhere in the Bible.

Question 1: Who was Melchizedek?

> Now this Melchizedek was a king over the land of Salem; and his people had waxed strong in iniquity and abomination; yea, they had all gone astray; they were full of all manner of wickedness;
>
> But Melchizedek having exercised mighty faith, and received the office of the high priesthood according to the holy order of God, did preach repentance unto his people. And behold, they did repent; and Melchizedek did establish peace in the land in his days; therefore he was called the prince of peace, for he was the king of Salem; and he did reign under his father.

Now, there were many before him, and also there were many afterwards, but none were greater; therefore, of him they have more particularly made mention. . . .

And it was this same Melchizedek to whom Abraham paid tithes; yea, even our father Abraham paid tithes of one-tenth part of all he possessed. (Alma 17:17–19, 15)

Question 2: How long has this higher priesthood been in existence?

This high priesthood being after the order of his Son [the Son of God], which order was from the foundation of the world; or in other words, being without beginning of days or end of years, being prepared from eternity to all eternity. (Alma 13:7)

This verse tells us that the higher priesthood after the order of the Son of God has been in existence since before the creation of the earth. In fact, it is the power by which God created the heavens and the earth. When Adam and Eve were cast out of the Garden of Eden, Adam built an altar upon which he offered sacrifices to the Lord. Because Adam could offer animal sacrifices, we know that Adam held this priesthood. Only an individual authorized by the Lord could perform such sacrifices.

Question 3: Why do God's children need the priesthood?

And again, my brethren, I would cite your minds forward to the time when the Lord God gave these commandments unto his children; and I would that ye should remember that the Lord God ordained priests, after his holy order, which was after the order of his Son, to teach these things unto the people.

And those priests were ordained after the order of his Son, in a manner that thereby the people might know in what manner to look forward to his Son for redemption. . . .

And thus being called by his holy calling, and ordained unto the high priesthood of the holy order of God, to teach his commandments unto the children of men, that they also might enter in his rest . . .

Now these ordinances were given after this manner, that thereby the people might look forward on the Son of God, it being a type of his order, or it being his order, and this that they might look forward to him for a remission of their sins, that they might enter into the rest of the Lord. (Alma 13:1–2, 6, 16)

There are ordinances of the gospel that are required for coming back into God's presence or to "enter into his rest," as Alma wrote. It is necessary that they be performed by men holding the proper authority to administer the ordinance. These ordinances include, among other things, baptism, the gift of the Holy Ghost, and sacrifice (anciently) and sacrament (today).

Question 4: How is a man determined to be worthy to hold this priesthood?

> And this is the manner after which they were ordained[5] . . . in the first place being left to choose good or evil; therefore they having chosen good, and exercising exceedingly great faith, are called with a holy calling, yea, with that holy calling which therefore they having chosen good, and exercising exceedingly great faith, are called with a holy calling . . .
>
> Now . . . there were many who were ordained and became high priests of God; and it was on account of their exceeding faith and repentance, and their righteousness before God, they choosing to repent and work righteousness rather than to perish. (Alma 13:3, 10)

In other words, these men show that, while they are not perfect, they are striving to live by God's commandment through faith and repentance and righteous service. These qualities are key to worthy priesthood service.

> And thus they have been called to this holy calling on account of their faith, while others would reject the Spirit of God on account of the hardness of their hearts and blindness of their minds, while, if it had not been for this they might have had as great privilege as their brethren. (Alma 13:4)

This is one of many scriptures that emphasizes that God doesn't bless some of His children and not others. No one is "predestined" to fail or to succeed. Alma teaches that all men have the same opportunity to qualify to hold the priesthood. It is through their own unrighteous choices that they are denied. There are many examples in the scriptures of men who tried to buy or usurp or change God's authority to their own condemnation.

Question 5: How is the priesthood conferred?

> Now they were ordained after this manner—being called with a holy calling, and ordained with a holy ordinance, and taking upon them the high priesthood of the holy order, which calling, and ordinance, and high priesthood, is without beginning or end—
>
> Thus they become high priests forever, after the order of the Son, the Only Begotten of the Father, who is without beginning of days or end of years, who is full of grace, equity, and truth. And thus it is. Amen. (Alma 13:8–9)

The priesthood is conferred by ordination and the laying on of hands by one holding the authority to ordain another to the priesthood.

Aaron and the Order of the Lesser Priesthood

In The Church of Jesus Christ of Latter-day Saints, we recognize two major divisions in the priesthood: the Aaronic or lesser priesthood and the Melchizedek or higher priesthood. This lesser priesthood was named after Aaron, the brother of Moses, for he was the first in Israel to be specifically ordained to this authority. In the Old Testament, it is also referred to as the Levitical Priesthood.

When the Lord spoke to Moses from the burning bush atop Mt. Sinai and called him to go to Egypt to free the enslaved Children of Israel, Moses was apprehensive. He feared that neither the Israelites nor Pharaoh would listen to him because he was slow of speech (Exodus 4:10). As a result, the Lord called Moses's brother Aaron, "the Levite," to be spokesman for him (Exodus 4:14–16).

After the Israelites were freed from Egypt, it became quickly apparent that years of slavery had taken their toll. The descendants of Israel were as immature as children. Their religious thinking was clouded by decades of exposure to the pagan gods of Egypt. They were as incapable of entering into the oath and covenant of the priesthood (see D&C 84:39–41) as an infant would be. Therefore, the Lord gave them the lesser law and preparatory ordinances (which became known as the law of Moses) and the lesser priesthood to administer those ordinances.

The Lord also knew that He could not confer the priesthood upon all the men of Israel, as had been the case under the patriarchs. Instead, He consecrated one tribe—the tribe of Levi—to be the ministers to all Israel. He further consecrated one family of Levites—the family of Moses's brother Aaron—to become the priests of Israel (see Exodus 28). They were washed, anointed, clothed in holy garments, and ordained to the priesthood (see Exodus 29). Others in the tribe of Levi were set apart to assist the priests. This lesser priesthood became known, as mentioned before, as the Levitical or Aaronic Priesthood.

It is important to note that no one takes priesthood authority upon himself. The Apostle Paul wrote of the priesthood that "no man taketh this honor unto himself, but he that is called of God, as was Aaron" (Hebrews 5:3). Jesus told His Apostles, "Ye have not chosen me, but I have chosen you, and ordained you" (John 15:16). Remember this point, because it is important throughout the history of God's relationship with His people.

A Worthy Priest of Aaron: John, Son of Zacharias, Priest of Aaron

Although Israel went through periods of apostasy in the hundreds of years from Moses to Jesus Christ, there were periods of time when the Aaronic Priesthood was on the Earth and was held among the descendants of Aaron. Eli, in the Old Testament, was a priest of the Levitical Priesthood when the boy Samuel was brought to him (1 Samuel 1:9, 25–28). Ezekiel was a priest living in captivity in Babylon when God called him to be a prophet (Ezekiel 1:3). Joshua was a high priest of Aaron when he was allowed to return to Jerusalem to help rebuild the temple following the Babylonian captivity (Ezra 2:2; this Joshua was a priest from the Babylonian captivity who returned to Jerusalem to serve as high priest). So, even when the people as a whole were unworthy, there often *were* worthy priesthood holders among them.

In the New Testament, we read of one such worthy Aaronic priest, a man named Zacharias. We know that he was a true descendant of Aaron because of the office he held. Men who were unable to document their lineage back to Aaron were denied the priesthood (Ezra 2:62). Zacharias's wife, Elizabeth, was also a descendant of Aaron (Luke 1:5). While there was a great deal of political chicanery going on in the office of the high priest and other temple leadership, there were worthy priesthood holders officiating in the temple. That Zacharias was one of these is evident from Luke's words that Zacharias and his wife were "righteous before God, walking in all the commandments and ordinances of the Lord blameless" (Luke 1:6).

Individual priests did not serve in the temple every day. They followed a scheduled course and may have served as infrequently as several days once a year. Whether they offered sacrifices or burned incense was determined by lot (Luke 1:8–9).

One day, when it was Zacharias's turn to serve in the temple, it was his lot to burn incense. While he was thus engaged, an angel appeared, standing just to the right of the altar of incense. The angel addressed him by name and told him that he and his wife would have a son, whom they should name John. He would be a chosen servant of the Lord from the womb, the forerunner chosen to prepare the way for the coming Messiah (Luke 1:11–17). Since both Zacharias and his wife were of advanced years, Zacharias questioned the validity of the angel's words. As a token of the promise, the angel gave him a sign: Zacharias would be struck dumb and unable to speak until all the words of the angel were fulfilled. When Zacharias emerged from the temple that day, all who knew him were amazed because he could not utter a single word (Luke 1:18–22).

True to the promise, Elizabeth conceived and the babe in her womb was filled with the Holy Ghost (Luke 1:15, 41). When the time came for her to deliver, a baby boy was born. All of the relatives immediately wanted to name him Zacharias after his father, even though Elizabeth insisted that he be called John.

Finally, someone handed Zacharias a tablet and asked him what he wanted to name his son. Zacharias wrote, "His name is John" (Luke 3:61–62). Immediately, Zacharias's mouth was opened, and he bore testimony of the miraculous events surrounding the announcement, conception, and birth of him who, in the spirit of an Elias or forerunner, would "be the voice of one crying in the wilderness, prepare ye the way of the Lord" (Luke 3:4).

We know very little of the childhood of John other than that he "waxed strong in spirit and was in the deserts till the day of his [showing] unto Israel"—which typically occurred at age thirty (Luke 1:80). John and Jesus were cousins, but we don't know if they spent time together.

We don't know much of John's childhood other than he grew up in the desert, dressed in camel's hair, and ate locusts and wild honey (Matthew 3:4; Mark 1:6). Jesus later accused the temple leadership of murdering John's father, Zacharias, "between the temple and the altar" (Matthew 23:35; Luke 11:51). The Prophet Joseph Smith taught that Zacharias, with a premonition of danger, sent John away to the mountains to protect him from whatever machinations ultimately cost him his own life.

All that we really know is that John, however he grew to manhood, had the authority to baptize, which was the authority of the Priesthood of Aaron, which he probably received from his father, most likely at a young age. Remember, John was also a literal descendant of Aaron. Even the Pharisees recognized John's authority as priest, although they did not act upon his call to repentance. John is best known as the man who baptized Jesus and who was later beheaded "at the instigation of Herodias."[6]

Understanding the Relationship between the Priesthood and Priesthood Keys

Priesthood is the authority to act in God's name, to minister to mankind, and administer saving ordinances. Priesthood keys constitute the authority to *direct* that work and to *confer* the priesthood upon others. What is often lost to our awareness is the fact that John was the last legal administrator to hold the keys of the Priesthood of Aaron for over 1800 years!

President Russell M. Nelson, when speaking to a group of young Aaronic Priesthood holders, taught about priesthood keys.[7] President Nelson, before he was called to full-time Church service, was a prominent heart surgeon. He used his experience as an analogy. Becoming a surgeon took years of preparation: college, medical school, internship, and residency. But even though he had several college degrees, including his MD, he could not legally practice medicine until he received that authority from those who held the "keys" to the practice of medicine—the State Board of Medical Examiners. Once licensed, he could practice medicine in his state within his field. He could not practice dentistry, chiropractic medicine, or neurosurgery. He also could not confer the right to practice medicine to other new MDs.

Here is an example of the appropriate use of priesthood keys using Elder Nelson's formula: Suppose a worthy man wants to baptize a family member or friend. Even though he holds the appropriate priesthood, he must receive authorization to do so from the bishop of the congregation because baptism is an Aaronic Priesthood ordinance and the bishop holds the keys to the Aaronic Priesthood ordinances for his congregation.

Jesus and the Priesthood

Jesus held the Melchizedek Priesthood (Hebrews 5:6). Paul tells us that Jesus was a high priest after the order of Melchizedek (Hebrews 4:15; 5:10). When He called the Twelve, He ordained them to the Melchizedek Priesthood and gave them the authority through that priesthood to serve as Apostles.[8]

The Keys of the Kingdom of Heaven

Even though Jesus was God—or perhaps *because* He was God—He respected and honored the priesthood keys held by righteous men such as Moses and Elijah.

Jesus promised His Apostles that He would give them "the keys of the kingdom of heaven: and whatsoever [they shall] bind on the Earth shall be bound in heaven: and whatsoever [they shall] loose on Earth shall be loosed in heaven" (Matthew 16:19). Within a week of that promise, Jesus took Peter, James, and John to a tall mountain, which has since become known as the Mount of Transfiguration. There, He received priesthood keys from Moses and Elijah and later gave them to the Apostles (Matthew 17:1–5).

The world has a hard time explaining what happened there and why. A modern-day revelation tells us that those men held specific priesthood keys: Moses, the keys to the gathering of Israel, and Elijah, the keys to the promised binding or sealing power.[9]

Jesus wanted His Apostles to have all the keys necessary for them to carry on the work of His Church following His death. The Apostles needed priesthood keys to organize branches of the Church, appoint and ordain local leaders, and pass on the holy Apostleship to others when one of them died. We know that they did this early in the young Church when they chose and ordained

Matthias to be an Apostle to take the place of Judas Iscariot, who had committed suicide after betraying Jesus (Acts 1:16–26).

Ordinances and Church Organization

According to the dictionary,[10] an ordinance is something believed to have been ordained by Deity. Ecclesiastically, it is an established rite or sacrament. There are forty-four references to the word *ordinance* in the King James Old Testament and only nine in the New Testament. But there are references to the performing of ordinances throughout the New Testament. There are eleven references regarding ordinances in the Book of Mormon and, like the New Testament, dozens of references of ordinances being performed.

One of the interesting things to note about the New Testament is that it is not a collection of gospel treatises set down as a definitive description of Jesus's Church. It is a collection of testimonies of Jesus's ministry (the four gospels); a historical record (Acts); a collection of letters of encouragement and warning (the epistles); and a great apocalyptic vision (Revelation). Because the epistles are primarily regulatory and not definitive, we are not on solid ground to accept the epistles as if they defined doctrine instead of simply reflecting it. If we want to look closely at ordinances and organization in the young Christian Church, we must study the New Testament carefully with that goal in mind.

The Priesthood and the Organization of Christ's Church

John 15:16 **Hebrews 5:6**	Jesus made it clear to his Apostles that they had not chosen Him, but that He had chosen them and ordained them. Paul reinforced this in his letter to the Hebrews. Righteous men are called and chosen to receive the priesthood and to hold Church offices. They do not seek those honors for themselves, but are called by one having authority, as was Aaron.
Acts 8:9–13, 18–20	Simon Magus, also known as the sorcerer, was impressed by the power he witnessed as Philip exercised his priesthood to heal the sick in Samaria. Simon was even baptized a Christian in hopes of gaining such power. But when he saw Peter and John confer the Holy Ghost, he was so impressed that he offered them money to buy the power he had seen them manifest. Peter rebuked him, saying, "Thy money perish with thee because thou has thought that the gift of God may be purchased with money." Priesthood authority cannot be bought or sold, nor can it be sought for personal gain or personal power.

Acts 1:16–26	Matthias was called and ordained an Apostle after the betrayal and suicide of Judas Iscariot. Men, like Judas, may lose their priesthood authority due to unrighteousness or death. When there is a vacancy in the Quorum of the Twelve Apostles, it is filled by the remaining Apostles after prayer and inspiration from the Holy Ghost.
2 Corinthians 12:11–12	All the Apostles were equal in authority. All held the Melchizedek Priesthood.
Luke 10:1	Jesus appointed righteous men to be seventies[11] and sent them forth, two by two, to preach the gospel. There are other priesthood offices to which men are called and ordained in the same manner as the Apostles were called and ordained. These seventy did not choose their position as missionaries; they were called to those positions by the Savior Himself.
Acts 6:1–6	Seven righteous men were called to care for the temporal needs of the Church so that the Apostles could focus on their primary responsibility to go forth, preach the gospel, and build the Church. Righteous priesthood holders can be called and set apart for other duties within the Church.
Acts 13:2–3	Paul and Barnabas were called and set apart before they set out on their first mission. Those who preach the gospel of Jesus Christ are called and given authority. They do not take the honor upon themselves.
1 Corinthians 12:28; Ephesians 2:19–20; Ephesians 4:11–13	Paul teaches the Corinthian and Ephesian Christians about priesthood offices and about how important it is that all exist in Christ's Church in the same way that all body parts are necessary for the body to function properly. Offices mentioned include the following: *prophets, Apostles, evangelists,*[12] *pastors,*[13] and *teachers.* These priesthood offices are to function for the "perfecting of the saints, for the work of the ministry, for the edifying of the body of Christ; till we all come in the unity of the faith, and of the knowledge of the Son of God, unto a perfect man." These are all priesthood offices. They were necessary in the young Christian Church and they are necessary today, according to Paul's definition of need. We are not perfect, neither as individuals nor as a Church collectively. We still need to be taught, ministered to, and edified. We have not achieved a unity of faith in the Christian Church. We still need these offices of the priesthood in the Church today.

1 Timothy 3:8–13; Titus 1:5	Paul instructed Timothy and Titus in the qualifications and responsibilities of deacons. The office of a deacon is a priesthood office. A deacon's primary responsibility was and is to help the bishop.
Acts 14:23; Acts 15:41; 1 Peter 5:1–4	The Apostles went forth to preach the gospel, and they called and ordained elders in every city to minister and administer the Church set up by the Savior in their various congregations. These local Church officers held the Melchizedek priesthood and served under the direction of the Apostles. The Apostles "confirmed"[14] the churches thus established. Elders were local Melchizedek Priesthood holders and they served in various capacities in the local congregations of the Church that Jesus Christ organized while He was on the earth.
1 Timothy 3:1–7; Titus 1:7–8	Paul instructed Timothy and Titus in the qualifications and responsibilities of bishops. Bishops held the primary authority to preside over local church organizations.

I began this book by reviewing the themes of the house of Israel and the covenants made between God and man. In this section I have disussed how these covenants, such as the Law of Sacrifice, often require the performance of a specific ordinance to fulfill the covenant. It is because ordinances are a part of God's dealings with His children that He has given to certain men the authority to act in His name in the performance of ordinances.

From the days of Moses until the coming of Jesus Christ, only a small portion of the house of Israel was given this priesthood power—the tribe of Levi.

During His life, Christ ordained a certain number of His followers to hold the higher priesthood after the order of Melchizedek, which priesthood He held. These men were also given the keys to the priesthood so that they could ordain others after the Savior's death. This continued until a great and universal apostasy came upon the Church of Jesus Christ, at which time priesthood authroity was lost. In the next theme, I will talk about apostasy and look into the reasons why it occurred, both in the Bible and in the Book of Mormon, and the consquences of such apostasy.

Notes

1.   Pronounced *Bah-all* with two syllables.
2.   See Appendix I: Patriarchal Genealogy from Adam to Abraham.

3. The Patriarchal Order of the Priesthood seems to have been lost in the generations following Jacob/Israel. If any of his sons held the priesthood, it is not firmly substantiated in scripture. It may be that Joseph did, based on the Book of Mormon notation that God renewed the Abrahamic Covenant with Joseph.

4. Daniel C. Peterson, *Where Have All the Prophets Gone?* (Springville, UT: Cedar Fort Publishing, 2005), 258, 268.

5. "To ordain" means to confer divine authority by the laying on of hands by one having the authority to do so.

6. Bible Dictionary, "John the Baptist."

7. Russell M. Nelson, "Keys of the Priesthood," *Ensign*, November 1987.

8. An *Apostle* is a priesthood office, as opposed to a *disciple*, who is any sincere follower of a wise leader—in this case, Jesus Christ.

9. The ancient prophets also restored their priesthood keys in these latter days to Joseph Smith in the Kirtland Temple in 1936 (see D&C 110:11–16).

10. *Merriam-Webster Online*, s.v. "ordinance," https://www.merriam-webster.com/dictionary /ordinance.

11. *Seventy* is a priesthood office, and those holding that office have the specific call to missionary work.

12. One who *tells forth*; the word is a twelfth-century word used to translate the original Hebrew; in the Church of Jesus Christ of Latter-day Saints, those who serve in an evangelical role are called patriarchs.

13. Ministers, pastors, and bishops.

14. *Confirm*: to make sure, to make official, to authorize

Recurring Cycles of Obedience, Disobedience, and Apostasy

Earlier, I discussed the fact that Lehi was told he would be led to a land "choice above all other lands." Like many of God's promises, this one is also made by covenant. In this theme, I will talk about what happens when mankind breaks its covenant promises to the Lord. How do people fall away from such a great promise? Are there gradual phases to the falling away so that the problem, if noted, can be corrected by repentance? Are there some who willfully rebel, knowing full well the nature of their choices? What can we do to catch our own individual straying from the covenant path in time to return and repent?

I have thus far discussed the importance of Israel and his descendants and about covenants God makes with those descendants. I discussed the priesthood and the necessary ordinances to witness to God our willingness to make those covenants with him. Lehi's promise is part of the Abrahamic Covenant: land, posterity, and being God's people. Lehi, as a descendant of Abraham through Jacob and Joseph, was promised a specific land. Lehi and his family were to be God's people—to have His commandments and His priesthood. If they kept God's commandments and honored and worshipped Him as their God, they would prosper in the land, both they and their posterity. If they did not, then God would withdraw His protection and leave them to experience the consequences of their own choices. It isn't that God delighted in punishing them; He loved them and wanted to bless them. But through disobedience, they tied His hands. He cannot bless His children in their sins any more than any parent could reward a child for deliberate disobedience lest the child think that wickedness brings happiness.

The Pride Cycle

Scholars of the Book of Mormon often refer to this as the pride cycle because pride and arrogance play such a huge part in the falling away from righteousness to sin. When the people remembered God and obeyed Him, they were blessed. As their blessings led them to prosperity, they often forgot God. They became prideful and claimed that their blessings were due solely to their own efforts. They began to mistreat their less fortunate neighbors and set up a social class system. They grew in disobedience.

As they became more disobedient and wicked, God withdrew His blessings and protection. They were left to experience the natural consequences of their own arrogant and wicked choices—consequences that were often very painful! If their suffering humbled them, they began to repent. They called upon God and promised to obey. If they were sincere and their actions showed true repentance, God would then be able to bless them again according to the covenant. If they didn't, their wickedness would lead them into individual and group apostasy, even to the degree that they would be destroyed as a people.

This cycle is seen throughout the Bible, particularly in the Old Testament, but nowhere is it more apparent than in the Book of Mormon. There are sixty examples of pride going before the Fall (see Proverbs 16:8) given in the Book of Mormon, so it is difficult to miss.[1] Because of the structure of the Bible, particularly the Old Testament, it is easy to miss. Once recognized from the Book of Mormon, it is far easier to find the pride cycle in the Bible. Why the *pride* cycle?[2] Because the sin of pride seems to be the root of all other sins. C. S. Lewis said that pride is the parent sin and all others spring from it. In his book *Mere Christianity,* he wrote, "The Christians are right: it is Pride which has been the chief cause of misery in every nation and every family since the world began. . . . Pride is always competitive. . . . Pride always means enmity—it is enmity. And not only enmity between man and man, but enmity to God."[3]

Cain and the Sin of Pride

The first falling away from God's commandments came very early in the human experience when Cain, in envy, killed his own brother to get gain, to take his brother's favored position, and in his pride to openly challenge God by changing His ordinance. Cain was jealous of his brother Abel, and he desired to have his brother's flocks. In the October General Conference of 1986, Elder Dallin H. Oaks said:

> Cain set the pattern of the world. Cain coveted the flocks of his brother Abel, and Satan showed him how to obtain them. Satan taught Cain that a man could get worldly wealth by committing some evil against its owner (JST, Gen. 5:16; Moses 5:31).[4]

What arrogance it must have taken to believe he could take his brother's wealth and his brother's life and God not know about it. When God asked him about his brother Cain, he lied and asked, "Am I my brother's keeper?" There was enmity between Cain and his brother, but more importantly, there was enmity toward God in Cain's heart. Because Cain knew the Lord so intimately, his consequences were dire indeed. This wasn't a casual misunderstanding or slipping away. It was willful and conscious rebellion. Just as Lucifer rebelled against God in the war in heaven, he covenanted with Cain and drew Cain into open rebellion toward God's sacred ordinance of sacrifice in the similitude of God's Only Begotten Son.

The Pride and Fall of the Children of Israel

There are many examples from the Old Testament of the Children of Israel turning from a life of obedience and blessing to a life of pride, selfishness, and sin. There are far too many examples to list them all, so I have selected some that I feel impressed to share.

Kings of Israel in the Old Testament

The Lord had set up the system of judges rather than calling a king. The Lord was to be their king. But the people wanted a king like the nations around them. The Lord allowed them to have kings, with predictable results. Their first king, Saul, was brought down to madness for his pride and jealousy. David, the second king, was brought down because of his lust and the prideful belief, like Cain, that somehow God wouldn't know when he committed adultery with Bathsheba and brought about the death of her husband, Uriah. Even wise Solomon, David's son, fell because he allowed his foreign wives to pollute his kingdom with images and worship of heathen gods, and his selfish arrogance in placing such a heavy tax burden upon his people to support his many wives and concubines, which burden was so crushing that his kingdom fractured upon his death.

A look at the kings of Israel after the division of the two kingdoms shows that there was not one single righteous king in Israel from Jeroboam to the fall of Israel before the Assyrians. There were only three such kings in Judah.[5] Among the Nephites there were great examples of good kings (Benjamin, Mosiah) and a terrible king (Noah). The Lord set up a system of judges among the Nephites after their last king, Mosiah, died. All four of his sons refused the throne in favor of missionary work and, thus, there was no successor, which was in fact a blessing.

When people are arrogant, prideful, selfish, and lazy, they are choosing a life outside of God's teachings. The Bible and the Book of Mormon are full of the stories of men and women who fell because of one or more of these weaknesses. Because we live in a fallen world, we are all subject to the magnetic power of these vices. Only through the conscious choice to love God and others can we hope to transcend our fallen state.

Scriptural Symbolism of a Fallen People

Here are examples given in the Old Testament that are symbolic of the ways in which the people fell. As you study them, look for pride, selfishness, or laziness at the root of the sin.

Israel as the Unfaithful Wife

One symbolic image the prophets used to describe Israel's backsliding was to picture Israel as the unfaithful wife and the Lord as the faithful husband. There are at least nine references in the Old Testament to Israel, such as this one "whoring after other gods" (Deuteronomy 31:6).

In truth, the Lord did not abandon Israel; she abandoned the Lord. Israel violated the covenant; the Lord did not. He withdrew only after Israel's sins were heavy. Isaiah prophesied before the downfall of Israel at the hands of the Assyrians.[6] Daniel prophesied similarly during the Babylonian conquest.[7]

Israel Believing That God Would Never Allow Them to Be Conquered

In the Old Testament, the Prophet Isaiah, who preached against the Northern Kingdom, wrote that the Samaritans were full of *pride* and *stoutness of heart*. Even though they had been frequently plagued by wars, they still felt in their arrogance that they could rebuild and be fine. They were wrong.[8]

Another example is found in the Book of Jeremiah. Judah was also arrogant and felt that the Lord would never allow another kingdom to destroy the Holy City (Jerusalem) or the Temple. Jeremiah had seen the Babylonian conquest in a vision and knew how wrong they were. He tried to warn them, citing the destruction of a healthy olive tree as a metaphor for Judah's inevitable destruction.[9]

Lehi also preached to Judah of her imminent demise at the hands of Babylon. His story is found in the first few chapters of the Book of Mormon, although his preaching began in Judah about the same time as Jeremiah.

The Lord's Pruning Away of the Rebellious from among the Righteous When They Fall

In Paul's epistle to the Romans, he spoke to the Roman Gentiles about the sin of pride. He compared them to the branches of the wild olive tree which were grafted into the tame tree (the house of Israel). Because of Israel's sins, many of her branches were broken off. He cautioned the Gentiles to "partake of the root and fatness of the olive tree," but not to become arrogant. If they fell subject to sin, they too would be cut off from the tree (Romans 11:17, 24; see the Book of Mormon version of the parable in Theme 1).

The Book of Mormon Explains the Symptoms of Apostasy

There are several key words that are found all over the Book of Mormon referring to the falling away of the people. Some of them slide into apostasy. Others openly rebel and turn completely away because of their pride, arrogance, and anger. One example of this happening was about two hundred years after the resurrection of Jesus Christ. During that time, the people had almost perfect peace and there were no poor among them. But in the two hundred and first year, the people began to change. Some behaviors described include

- being lifted in pride
- wearing costly apparel and jewelry
- desiring the fine things of the world
- dividing into social classes
- denying God's gospel as it had been taught them and
- building up churches to themselves to get financial gain[10]
- offering sacraments and sacred ordinances in their churches to people who were not worthy to receive; thus, the people ate and drank damnation to their souls
- persecuting those who believed in Jesus and His original Church
- imprisoning believers and, eventually, seeking to kill them as had been done in Jerusalem

After just thirty years, the people's hearts were so hardened that they again divided into Nephites and Lamanites—a group that willfully and with malice aforethought turned away from the Lord and all He represented (see 4 Nephi 1).

The people continued to harden their hearts until, in about AD 400, their hearts were so hardened that they were no longer capable of repentance. Those years were marked by continued and worsened wickedness. There was constant warfare and carnage. The Prophet Mormon was called at the young age of ten years to abridge one thousand years of Nephite records, writing only those things which were most important on thin metal sheets.

By then, both the Nephites and the Lamanites were wicked to such a degree that is rarely found among God's people. Both sides participated in murder, rape, human sacrifice, and cannibalism. It is little wonder that God withdrew His hand and allowed them to destroy themselves! The once-proud Nephites were annihilated by their enemies; even the prophet Mormon died. Only his son Moroni survived to carry Mormon's abridged records to a place of safety. It is through Moroni that we now have access to those records in the Book of Mormon. He and his father witnessed the downfall of an entire nation through pride and sin. By preserving their eyewitness record of the fruits of apostasy, they teach us to look for the seeds of apostasy in the small things before they grow into a tangled vine of spiritual destruction.

Such were the fruits of apostasy in the Old Testament and the Book of Mormon—Israel destroyed and scattered by the Assyrians; Judah destroyed and carried away by the Babylonians; Nephites annihilated by their enemies, the Lamanites. It seems as if people are slow to heed the words of God; we need to remember the sweet fruits of obedience and the bitter fruits of apostasy. If we ever wonder if something, some person, or some group is leading us astray, we should look to the fruits. "By their fruits ye will know them" (Matthew 7:20).

The New Testament: Usurped Authority and Apostasy

I will now turn my attention to the New Testament. As we see from the final books of the Old Testament, the Jews were returned to Jerusalem by the king of Persia, where they rebuilt the temple. During those intertestamental years, there were many ups and downs in the pride cycle among the Jews. By the time of Jesus's birth, the House of David was no longer in power. The Maccabean family had ruled for generations until an Idumean named Herod married the daughter of the Maccabees in 38 BC and became the 'king' of the Kingdom of Judea as a vassal to the Roman Empire. This was the family in power at the time of Christ's birth. They were not Jews but rather so-called *converts* to Judaism, driven by power and greed.

Most Christians are familiar with the story of Jesus cleansing the temple in Jerusalem. All four gospel writers recorded such an event. The temple in Jerusalem was a massive structure covering the entire Temple Mount.

There was a huge court surrounding the temple that was called the Court of the Gentiles, which anyone could enter. The inner courts were restricted, in order, to women, men, and priests, leading ultimately to the Holy of Holies into which only the high priest could enter. While there were varying degrees of "holiness," for lack of a better word, the entire Temple Mount within the walls was considered God's house and, therefore, sacred.

So as not to pollute God's holy house, Herod built stalls beneath the temple itself where sacrificial animals could be examined or sold and where patrons could change their gentile money (which bore Caesar's image—a violation of the second of the Ten Commandments) for the temple shekels.

When Jesus entered the temple court during the Passover, the first things He saw were the money changers and the animal stalls—*in* the court of the temple, not *under* it! That in and of itself would have been enough to anger Him, but He knew that commerce could not be taking place within the temple without at least the tacit approval of the high priest and the temple leadership. I believe that *this* was the true sticking point for the Savior: the usurped authority being exercised by men who were not true priests of Aaron.

While there was at least one honorable and legitimate Aaronic priest serving in the temple (Zacharias), the high priest and temple leaders were neither honorable nor legitimate. Aaron's descendants had continued as high priests until about 175 BC, when the position became one of political appointment. When Herod came into power in Judea in 37 BC, he also appointed whomever he chose to be high priest regardless of parentage or line of authority—this in total disregard of Mosaic law.

At the time of Jesus's mission, the high priest was a man named Joseph Caiaphas. His father-in-law, Annas, had served before him, and the two frequently colluded on temple matters,[11] even though there was supposed to be only one serving as high priest at a time.

Jesus knew that these men held no legitimate priesthood authority and the buying and selling of animals, money-changing, and other unholy actions were going on in the temple with their knowledge and, perhaps, even at their instigation. Those activities became a living representation of the dishonesty and apostasy in the temple leadership.

When Jesus said, "It is written, 'My house is a house of prayer:' but ye have made it a den of thieves," He wasn't referring only to the money-changers (Matthew 21:13; Luke 19:48). He was also referring to Caiaphas and Annas and others of the temple hierarchy. We know this because the Greek word that is translated in the King James Bible as *thieves* can also mean *usurpers*. That word was not lost on Caiaphas and Annas. I believe the conspiracy to kill Jesus began the day of the first temple cleansing and solidified at the second cleansing. Jesus had looked beneath their masks of propriety and had exposed them as usurping authority that was not rightfully theirs. Jesus could not be allowed to live because He knew and proclaimed the temple leadership to be corrupt and apostate.

The Great Apostasy

In an earlier chapter, I talked about the priesthood of God and the importance of having it upon the earth. Priesthood is necessary for the ordinances required to return to Heavenly Father and find exaltation in His kingdom. Jesus gave the priesthood of Melchizedek to his Apostles; He founded His Church upon a foundation of Apostles and prophets (see Ephesians 20:20). There were other priesthood offices, such as elders and bishops and deacons (see Ephesians 4:11). He taught baptism by immersion by both precept and example (see Matthew 3:13; John 3:5). He instituted the ordinance of the sacrament to replace the Mosaic Law of Sacrifice (see Luke 22:19). He received the keys to the priesthood on the Mount of Transfiguration and passed them on to his Apostles so that they would have all the authority they needed after He was gone from their presence (see Matthew 16:19; Mark 9:2). He promised them the companionship of the Comforter in His absence (see John 14:16; Acts 2:4).

What happened to the priesthood the Apostles held? Why was there a "falling away" prophesied by the Apostles themselves (2 Thessalonians 2:3)? How were the fundamental truths of the gospel so altered and polluted that by the fourth century AD, the Church was almost unrecognizable from the Christianity of the New Testament?

Three factors contributed to what became known as the Great Apostasy:

1. Severe persecution of the Christians by the Roman Empire and by other political and religious groups of the day.
2. Travel conditions of the day that made taking care of Church business and ordaining new priesthood offices, including that of Apostles and bishops, difficult.
3. Heresy and apostasy from within the Church itself.[12]

Persecution from Rome

One by one, the Apostles and other righteous priesthood leaders were martyred.[13] The only one who wasn't slain was John the Beloved, who was banished to a penal colony on the Isle of Patmos by the Emperor Domitian. He was later released and returned to his home in Ephesus. The ancient historian Hippolytus wrote that "he fell asleep at Ephesus, where his remains were sought for but could not be found."[14] Scripture tells us that John did *not* die but was translated to remain upon the earth until the Savior comes again (see John 21:22–23, D&C 7:1–3). Without living Apostles to ordain others to the priesthood, as the ordained bishops and other Church leaders died off, the priesthood ceased to exist. Remember that bishops held the keys to their particular office as local authorities, but they did not have the keys to pass on that priesthood to others. For example, one bishop was no more powerful than any other, and no bishop could call and ordain anothor bishop. Thus, as rightfully ordained priesthood leaders died, it left a void because there were no general Church authorities who held the keys to call and ordain other men to the priesthood.

Travel Conditions in the Ancient World

When serious questions arose in the Church, the Apostles met to discuss the issues and to pray for inspiration from God. The first known conference of the Apostles is described in the book of Acts and occurred in Jerusalem. It was convened primarily to discuss the question of baptizing Gentiles without their first being circumcised. Paul traveled home from his first mission to attend that conference because he and Barnabus encountered that situation frequently. Peter, who was the senior Apostle, spoke out against requiring circumcision. When the final decision was made, letters were prepared and sent to all the branches of the Church informing them of the official Church policy (see Acts 15:22–29).

Even though the Romans had constructed an excellent system of roads through their empire, most travel still occurred by foot. Due to the difficulty and time involved in travel and communication, as the Apostles were killed one by one, it became difficult for them to meet in conference to address the questions of false doctrine that were mushrooming everywhere. They wrote against such heresies in their epistles, but their words were not always accepted by the members. Even with the good system of roads that existed in the Roman Empire, the burden of traveling to organize the Church and call local priesthood leaders, to regulate the Church when it was being led astray by heretical ideas, and to call and ordain new Apostles to replace those who had died eventually fell upon increasingly fewer Apostles until none were left but John.[15]

Apostasy from within the Church

The biggest threat to the young Church didn't come from Rome; it came from a deliberate apostasy from within the Church. Speaking of the Second Coming of Jesus, Paul wrote to the Thessalonians: "Let no man deceive you by any means: for that day shall not come, except there be a falling away first" (2 Thessalonians 2:3). The Greek word that translates as *falling away* has the same root as the Greek word *apostasis*. That word in English is *apostasy*.

Jesus allowed John to stay upon the earth in part so that priesthood keys would remain among men. But that was predicated upon men being willing to acknowledge John's leadership as the last living Apostle. In one of his own letters, John wrote that one branch of the Church had refused to receive him or any other duly authorized priesthood leader (see 3 John 1:9–10). When that spirit of apostasy became prevalent, John was taken out of their midst.

John wasn't the only Apostle to see the members departing from pure doctrine. In the epistles, there are at least twenty-four different occasions where an Apostle accused one of the branches of the Church of apostasy.[16]

Apostolic Warnings Found in the New Testament Foretelling the Great Apostasy

The Apostle Peter

> But there were false prophets also among the people, even as there shall be false teachers among you, who privily shall bring in damnable heresies, even denying the Lord that bought them, and bring upon themselves swift destruction.
>
> And many shall follow their pernicious ways; by reason of whom the way of truth shall be evil spoken of. (2 Peter 2:1–2)

The Apostle John

> Little children, it is the last time: and as ye have heard that antichrist shall come, even now are there many antichrists . . .
>
> They went out from us, but they were not of us; for if they had been of us, they would no doubt have continued with us: but they went out, that they might be made manifest that they were not all of us. (1 John 2:18–19)

> For many deceivers are entered into the world, who confess not that Jesus Christ is come in the flesh.[17] This is a deceiver and an antichrist. . . .
>
> Whosoever transgresseth, and abideth not in the doctrine of Christ, hath not God. He that abideth in the doctrine of Christ, he hath both the Father and the Son.
>
> If there come any unto you, and bring not this doctrine, receive him not into your house, neither bid him God speed. (2 John 1:7, 9–10)

I wrote unto the church: but Diotrephes, who loveth to have the preeminence among them, receiveth us not.

Wherefore, if I come, I will remember his deeds which he doeth, prating against us with malicious words: and not content therewith, neither doth he himself receive the brethren, and forbiddeth them that would, and casteth them out of the church. (3 John 1:9–10)

The Apostle Paul

For I know this, that after my departing shall grievous wolves enter in among you, not sparing the flock. Also of your own selves shall men arise, speaking perverse things, to draw away disciples after them. (Acts 20:29)

For when for the time ye ought to be teachers, ye have need that one teach you again which be the first principles of the oracles of God; and are become such as have need of milk, and not of strong meat.[18] (Hebrews 5:12)

But if any man seem to be contentious, we have no such custom, neither the churches of God . . .

For first of all, when ye come together in the church, I hear that there be divisions among you; and I partly believe it.

For there must be also heresies among you, that they which are approved may be made manifest among you. (1 Corinthians 11:16, 18–19)

I marvel that ye are so soon removed from him that called you into the grace of Christ unto another gospel:

Which is not another; but there be some that trouble you, and would pervert the gospel of Christ. (Galatians 1:6–7)

O foolish Galatians, who hath bewitched you, that ye should not obey the truth, before whose eyes Jesus Christ hath been evidently set forth, crucified among you? (Galatians 3:1)

Let no man deceive you by any means: for that day shall not come, except there come a falling away first, and that man of sin be revealed, the son of perdition. (2 Thessalonians 2:3)

Neither give heed to fables and endless genealogies,[19] which minister questions, rather than godly edifying which is in faith: so do.

Now the end of the commandment is charity, out of a pure heart, and of a good conscience, and of faith unfeigned:

From which some having swerved have turned aside unto vain jangling;

Desiring to be teachers of the law; understanding neither what they say, nor whereof they affirm.[20] (1 Timothy 1:4–7)

Now the Spirit speaketh expressly, that in the latter times[21] some shall depart from the faith, giving heed to seducing spirits, and doctrines of devils;

Speaking lies in hypocrisy; having their conscience seared with a hot iron;

Forbidding to marry, and commanding to abstain from meats,[22] which God hath created to be received with thanksgiving of them which believe and know the truth. (1 Timothy 4:1–3)

This thou knowest, that all they which are in Asia[23] be turned away from me; . . .

But shun profane and vain babblings: for they will increase unto more ungodliness.

And their word will eat as doth a canker; . . .

Who concerning the truth have erred, saying that the resurrection is past already; and overthrow the faith of some. (2 Timothy 1:15; 2:16–18)

For men shall be lovers of their own selves, covetous, boasters, proud, blasphemers, disobedient to parents, unthankful, unholy,

Without natural affection, trucebreakers, false accusers, incontinent, fierce, despisers of those that are good,

Traitors heady, highminded, lovers of pleasures more than lovers of God;

Having a form of godliness, but denying the power[24] thereof: from such turn away . . .

Ever learning, and never able to come to the knowledge of the truth.

Now as Jannes and Jambres withstood Moses, so do these also resist the truth: men of corrupt minds, reprobate concerning the faith.

But they shall proceed no further: for their folly shall be manifest unto all men, as theirs also was. (2 Timothy 3:2–5, 7–9)

For the time will come when they will not endure sound doctrine; but after their own lusts shall they heap to themselves teachers, having itching ears[25];

And they shall turn away their ears from the truth, and shall be turned unto fables. (2 Timothy 4:3–4)

For there are many unruly and vain talkers and deceivers, specially they of the circumcision[26]:

Whose mouths must be stopped, who subvert whole houses[27] . . .

This witness is true. Wherefore rebuke them sharply, that they may be sound in the faith;

Not giving heed to Jewish fables, and commandments of men, that turn from the truth.

Unto the pure all things are pure: but unto them that are defiled and unbelieving is nothing pure; but even their mind and conscience is defiled.

They profess that they know God; but in works they deny him, being abominable, and disobedient, and unto every good work reprobate. (Titus 1:10–11, 13–16)

The Apostle Jude

For there are certain men crept in unawares, who were before of old ordained to this condemnation, ungodly men, turning the grace of our God into lasciviousness,[28] and denying the only Lord God, and our Lord Jesus Christ. . . .

But these speak evil of those things which they know not: but what they know naturally, as brute beasts, in those things they corrupt themselves.

Woe unto them! . . .

To execute judgment upon all, and to convince all that are ungodly among them of all their ungodly deeds which they have ungodly committed, and of all their hard speeches which ungodly sinners have spoken against him.

These are murmurers, complainers, walking after their own lusts; and the mouth speaketh great swelling word, having men's persons in admiration because of advantage[29] . . .

These be they who separate themselves,[30] sensual, having not the Spirit. (Jude 1:4, 10–11, 15–16, 19)

But, beloved, remember ye the words which were spoken before of the Apostles of our Lord Jesus Christ;

How that they told you there should be mockers in the last time, who should walk after their own ungodly lusts. (Jude 1:17–18)

Jude summed it up when he reminded Church members what all of the Apostles had warned against—not just physical lust, but *lusts*, plural: money, power, authority, prestige, popularity, control, revenge, and all unworthy desires. By the time the Apostles died, many Christians had forgotten their wise counsel. "Twilight had passed and the dark night of apostasy was upon them."[31] Jude's summary of the seeds of apostasy—money, power, authority, prestige, popularity, control, and revenge, along with pride—is very reminiscent of those things described by Mormon in his lifetime.

Anti-Christs and Their Role in Apostasy

Many people think there will be one anti-Christ in the future. However, the New Testament Apostles spoke of having many anti-Christs already in the young Church, leading members astray with false doctrine, Greek philosophies, and the law. Anti-Christs are those who are

- teaching things they ought not teach (Titus 1:11)[32]
- Not willing to endure sound doctrine (2 Timothy 4:3)
- following their own lusts (1 Timothy 3)
- heaping to themselves teachers, having itching ears (2 Timothy 4:3)
- turning away from the truth; believing fables (2 Timothy 4:3; Titus 1:7, 11; 1 Peter 5:2)
- preaching for filthy lucre's sake (1 Timothy 3)
- speaking profane, vain babblings (2 Timothy 2:16)
- departing from the faith (1 Timothy 4:1)
- giving heed to seducing spirits (2 Timothy 2:16)
- teaching doctrines of devils (2 Timothy 2:16)
- speaking lies in hypocrisy (1 Timothy 4:2)
- perverting the gospel of Christ (Galatians 1:7)
- false prophets (2 Peter 2:1)
- heeding false teachers (2 Peter 2:1)
- accepting damnable heresies, pernicious ways (2 Peter 2:1)

Paul called them "grievous wolves among the flock" (Acts 20: 29) and John called them "deceivers and antichrist" (2 John 1:7) who "shall come, even now are there many anti-Christs" (1 John 2:18). These pronouncements are very clear to those who study the New Testament looking for them. Some of those anti-Christs are singled out by name in the epistles, although we don't know much about them as individuals.

There are several anti-Christs named in the Book of Mormon, and we do know quite a bit about them. President Ezra Taft Benson once wrote: "The Book of Mormon brings men to Christ through two basic means. First, it tells in a plain manner of Christ and His gospel . . . Second, The Book of Mormon exposes the enemies of Christ . . . It fortifies the humble followers of Christ against the evil designs, strategies, and doctrines of the devil in our day."[33]

An anti-Christ is defined as anyone or anything that actively opposes Jesus Christ—either openly or secretly. As mentioned earlier, when most people talk about *the* anti-Christ, they are referring to the servant of the "beast" described in the Book of Revelation who is to come. While this is the most common use of the word, in truth, there have been anti-Christs in the world ever since Cain. The scriptures and the pages of history are full of such references.

One of the Book of Mormon anti-Christs had an immense negative impact on the Nephites. His name was Nehor.[34] At his trial, the prophet Alma accused Nehor of introducing priestcraft among his people. Here is a short comparison between usurped and unauthorized priestcraft and God's priesthood.

Priesthood	*Priestcraft*
1. Jesus Christ is the light and focus of the preaching.	1. The man who is preaching is the focus of attention.
2. Those holding the priesthood are humble and don't seek personal popularity.	2. Those involved in priestcraft seek personal popularity, becoming prideful and arrogant.
3. Priesthood holders seek only the welfare of the people and the building up of God's kingdom on earth.	3. Those who practice priestcraft seek their own personal welfare: riches, fame, and power.

Watch for priestcraft when looking for an anti-Christ. A thorough look through scripture shows example after example of priestcraft, from the Ba'al worship in the Old Testament to men like Simon Magus in the New Testament. It takes the Book of Mormon, however, to highlight the underlying attributes and attraction of priestcraft so that we, as readers, can be forewarned against multiple examples of priestcraft. In our world, even today, priestcraft is leading many people astray.

In summary, I have looked at the circle of blessings, pride, sin, suffering, and repentance of the pride cycle. I've shown examples in ancient Israel and the ultimate destruction of the apostate people in the Old Testament. I looked at examples of anti-Christs in the New Testament, several of whom are called out by name in the epistles of the Apostles, and I've shown the havoc they have wrought that brought such divisiveness in the early Church that led to the loss of truth and priesthood by the third century AD. Finally, I have shown very clear examples of the specific ways anti-Christs lead people away for the very Savior who could heal and bless them.

These scriptural stories are cautionary tales for us. The anti-Christs of today are very persuasive. Corrupt judges and lawyers, such as some of the Nephite judges or the Pharisees, who stirred contention to get gain, live among us. You cannot watch the news of the world without seeing them, but often we fail to recognize them for who and what they are: liars and the servants of the father of lies. As disciples of Jesus Christ, we need to avoid them when possible and testify of God's truth to counter their lies lest we fall into individual apostasy as well as societal apostasy.

Notes

1. Joe J. Christensen, "Pride—The 'Parent Sin,'" *Ensign*, June 1974.
2. See Appendix E: The Pride Cycle.
3. Lewis, C. S., *Mere Christianity*, retrieved from http://www.timesandseasons.org/The _Great_Sin_condensed.pdf.
4. Dallin H. Oaks, "Brother's Keeper," *Ensign*, November 1986.
5. See Appendix J: Kings of Israel and Judah.
6. "Thus saith the Lord, Where is the bill of your mother's divorcement, whom I have put away? Or which of my creditors is it to whom I have sold you? Behold, for your iniquities have you sold yourself, and for your transgressions is your mother put away" (Isaiah 50:1).
7. "We have sinned, and have committed iniquity, and have done wickedly, and have rebelled, even by departing from the precepts and from thy judgments" (Daniel 9:5).
8. "Therefore the Lord will cut off from Israel head and tail, branch and rush, in one day" (Isaiah 9:14).
9. "The Lord called thy name, A green, olive tree, fair, and of goodly fruit: with the noise of a great tumult he hath kindled fire upon it, and the branches of it are broken" (Jeremiah 11:16).
10. In the true Church of Jesus Christ, there is no paid clergy because that does lead to pride and dissension.
11. These are the men before whom Jesus was later tried. They were the instigators of the cry: "Crucify him."
12. When I refer to the Universal or Catholic Church, I do so from a historical perspective. The Catholic Church today has undergone several reform movements and is different in many ways from the early church I discuss here.
13. See Appendix K: Fate of the Apostles.
14. Scott R. Peterson, *Where Have All the Prophets Gone?* (Springville, UT: Cedar Fort, 2005), 115–17. Many historical references regarding the apostasy and reformation come from this book. It is a well-researched, carefully documented, and scholarly work, and I highly recommend it to any faithful and concerned Christian.
15. It amazes me that these remarkable men were able to travel as far and as much as they did. They went south into Africa, east as far as India, north into Russia, west to Spain, and northwest to Western Europe and England.
16. Dr. Noah Reynolds, *Messiah: Behold the Lamb of God*, PBS, BYUTV.
17. A philosophy known as *Docetism* coming primarily from Greek philosophy that the physical body was corrupt and imperfect and that, therefore, a god would never possess a physical body.
18. The branch at Jerusalem was the oldest branch of the Church, begun during the Savior's lifetime. They should have been leading out in teaching and living the gospel, but by the time Paul wrote to them, they were as immature in the gospel as new converts. Part of the problem was that the Jewish Christians kept reverting back to the old traditions of the law of Moses. Scholars refer to them as the *Judaizers*.
19. Simon Magus, who tried to buy the priesthood from Peter, left the Church and formed an apostate group that led away many early Christians. He invented a story, complete with an elaborate genealogy, showing that he was higher on the family tree of God than Jesus and that, while Jesus was a good man who taught many good things, those who

followed Simon were in possession of secret ideas that made them closer to the Father. Remember that Simon was a sorcerer and undoubtedly received inspiration to make his lies seem convincing from the Father of Lies, the "god" he really worshipped. Simon wanted personal power and aggrandizement and was the father of the Gnostic movement.

20. Men were setting themselves up as teachers when they themselves didn't know what they were talking about and the people were heeding them and ignoring the Apostles.

21. Some read this to mean the last days—our day. While these conditions do exist today, they had already begun in the days of the Apostles. To Paul, the latter day meant the near future, as he names four specific men already teaching false doctrine.

22. Both these conditions occurred in the Universal Church by the fourth century.

23. This refers to the Church in Turkey, one of the earliest branches of the Church.

24. These men did not recognize authorized priesthood authority and had begun to deny the need for the priesthood.

25. Men who seek out preachers who tell them what they want to hear so that they may feel justified in continuing to do whatever they want, not what God wants of them.

26. The Judaizers.

27. Paid clergy of apostate offshoot churches; there was and is no paid clergy in Jesus Christ's true Church.

28. Some were teaching that since grace saves, all someone had to do was to become a Christian and then he could do whatever he wanted. There was a lot of sexual immorality among the early Church with the idea that it was okay because Jesus paid for their sins. Paul addressed this issue in his letters to the Romans and Corinthians. One example from Romans 6: "Shall we continue in sin that grace may abound? God forbid!" (v. 1–2).

29. People listened to men of prominence and wealth, even though those men were not righteous men or duly ordained Church leaders—much in the same way that we often admire movie stars and sports heroes, even when those people often live immoral lives and more often don't know whereof they speak.

30. Apostatize or leave the Church.

31. Dr. Kent Brown, *Messiah: Behold the Lamb of God,* a PBS Production, presented by BYUTV, 2010.

32. Paul's letters to Titus and Timothy are giving counsel as to the behavior and character of those who hold priesthood offices, most particularly bishops and deacons.

33. Benson, Ezra Taft. "The Book of Mormon is the Word of God," *Ensign,* January 1988.

34. See Appendix C: Anti-Christs in the Book of Mormon for more information about Nehor and other such self-appointed teachers who seduced the people with their false doctrine.

THEME 5

The Creation and the Fall: Agency, Opposition, and Accountability

I n the first three themes, I have discussed the house of Israel, the unifying thread of God's people that weaves throughout history. I talked about the importance of sacred covenants and the role ordinances play in making solemn covenants with God. I then discussed the importance of the priesthood and why God gives certain men the authority to act in His name in performing ordinances and carrying on the organization of His Church here on earth. In the last theme, I looked at what happens when people keep their covenants and, likewise, what happens when they don't. I spoke of the pride cycle and how failing to repent can lead to individual and group apostasy.

In this theme, I will look at the creation of the world and the Fall of Adam and Eve, as well as how the Fall gave mankind agency and accountability. I will also look at how the original *curses* in the Garden allow opposition in all things, which is necessary for men and women to grow strong.

The late Bruce R. McConkie of the Quorum of the Twelve Apostles spoke of the Creation and the Fall as two of what he called *the Three Pillars of Eternity* (the Atonement being the third). In an oft-quoted devotional address, given at Brigham Young University in 1981, he said:

> If we can gain an understanding of them, then the whole eternal scheme of things will fall into place, and we will be in a position to work out our salvation. . . .
>
> These three are the foundations upon which all things rest. Without any one of them all things would lose their purpose and meaning, and the plans and designs of Deity would come to naught.[1]

The Creation

> In the beginning God created the heaven and the earth. (Genesis 1:1)

This is the first sentence in the text we know as the Bible. The first chapter of this very first book goes on to describe the six creative periods of Earth's existence. Some people interpret the use of the word *day* as meaning twenty-four-hours. I have issues with this, since creating the earth and placing it in its orbit happened during one of these creative periods indicates to me that twenty-four-hour days didn't exist in the early stages of creation. Thomas R. Valletta of the Ogden Utah Institute of Religion wrote in answer to a question in a Church magazine in 1994 the following:

> Latter-day Saints have additional information that allows a [different] view: that each 'day' of the Creation was of unspecified duration, and that the creation of the earth took place during an unknown length of time. In fact, Abraham stresses that *time* is synonymous with day. . . . This usage is completely consistent with the ancient Hebrew. The Hebrew word, YOM, often translated "day," can also mean "time" or "period." In other words, the term translated day in Genesis could be appropriately read as period.[2]

Jehovah, the premortal Jesus Christ, was the Creator. All scripture testifies of this:

> Hast thou not known? hast thou not heard, that the everlasting God, the Lord, the Creator of the ends of the earth. (Isaiah 40:28)

> In the beginning was the Word,[3] and the Word was with God, and the Word was God. The same was in the beginning with God. All things were made by him; and without him was not anything made that was made. (John 1:3)

> And he shall be called Jesus Christ, the Son of God, the Father of heaven and earth, the Creator of all things from the beginning. (Mosiah 3:8)

Toward the end of the sixth creative period, the Gods[4] created mankind. The Hebrew word *adam* means *man* or *mankind*. Adam was both his name and a description of who he was, the father of all living. That is why the creation story teaches us that the Gods "created man in his own image, in the image of God created he him: male and female created he them" (Genesis 1:27). The first commandment God gave to Adam and Eve was to multiply and replenish the earth. Afterward, God showed them the Garden, explaining that everything created was for their benefit and that they were responsible to care for the Garden. Then God explained:

Of every tree of the garden thou mayest freely eat:

But of the tree of knowledge of good and evil, thou shalt not eat of it: for in the day that thou eatest thereof thou shalt surely die. (Genesis 2:16–17)

In that short statement—just one and a half verses of Genesis—something remarkable and of utmost importance happened. Latter-day revelation makes it clear that God pointed out to Adam and Eve that they should not eat *if* they wanted to stay in the Garden. But from the beginning, He gave them the final choice. In the Garden, God gave mankind his agency, the most important gift next to the gift of life itself.[5]

The Fall

Most of the world has a very different view of the Fall than The Church of Jesus Christ of Latter-day Saints. For centuries, churches have believed and taught that what happened in Eden was the original sin. This led to centuries of unequal treatment of women because Eve was the first to partake. Eve has long been seen as an almost witless sinner who heeded Satan's beguiling and Adam as a hapless victim of Eve's wiles. Nothing could be further from the truth. Scholar Beverly Campbell in her book *Eve and the Choice Made in Eden* explains that the ancient Hebrew word that translates as *beguiled* is far richer, deeper, and complex than our modern translation suggests.[6] It means that the serpent explained a great deal to Eve and she pondered her choices and the effects they would have. She knew she and Adam were to have children. She also knew they could not do that if they remained in an immortal state in Eden. She transgressed a lesser commandment to keep a much higher law. How different the world would have been for millennia if Eve had been seen as the courageous heroine she was instead of a beguiling temptress who led her poor husband into sin!

Why did Eve partake when Adam wouldn't? Did God know she would be the first to partake and, of necessity, move Adam to partake? I don't know that anyone but God knows that. However, what we do know is that when God created mankind, He created the male and female brains differently. I found this quote from *Psychology Today* magazine. I found it interesting in terms of the way men and women process information.

Male brains utilize nearly seven times more *gray matter* for activity while female brains utilize nearly ten times more *white matter*. What does this mean?

Gray matter areas of the brain are localized. They are information- and action-processing centers in specific splotches in a specific area of the brain.

This can translate to a kind of tunnel vision when they are doing something. Once they are deeply engaged in a task or game, they may not demonstrate much sensitivity to other people or their surroundings.

White matter is the networking grid that connects the brain's gray matter and other processing centers with one another. This profound brain-processing difference . . . may explain why, in adulthood, females are great multi-taskers, while men excel in highly task-focused projects.[7]

Could that be why Eve was able to think broadly and thus was able to understand clearly the eternal implications of her choice? We don't know, and it really isn't important to know. For me, it presents a possible scenario that helps me understand our first parents better. When Satan tempted Eve by telling her that she would not die immediately, but would know good from evil, he thought he was thwarting God's plan. In fact, he was furthering God's plan. When Eve *saw* the tree (Genesis 3:6), she *saw* it as God sees it and understood clearly what she would have to do for mankind to progress beyond a state of perpetual innocence to the understanding of right and wrong and the agency to act upon that understanding.

President Joseph Fielding Smith once said:

Adam did only what he had to do. He partook of that fruit for one good reason, and that was to open the door to bring you and me and everyone else into this world, for Adam and Eve could have remained in the Garden of Eden; they could have been there to this day, if Eve hadn't done something.[8]

Professor Robert L. Millet, then Dean of Religious Education at Brigham Young University, wrote about the Fall of Adam and Eve in an article in the *Ensign*. I love the way he explains the difference between the way most of the world views our first parents, particularly Eve, from the way Latter-day Saints see them. He wrote:

The Latter-day Saint view of the scenes in Eden is remarkably optimistic when compared to traditional Christian views. We believe that Adam and Eve went into the Garden of Eden to fall, . . . that the Fall was as much a part of the foreordained plan of the Father as the very Atonement. . . we look upon what Adam and Eve did with great appreciation rather than with disdain.[9]

Agency

Why would God put His children in such a position of having to choose between two commandments? Latter-day revelation helps us recognized the *why* of this question.

Today, many churches are teaching the *Fortunate Fall*—in other words, that it was a good thing that Eve and, ultimately, Adam did what they did. However, the term *fortunate fall* almost seems to imply that God was bringing something good out of a bad situation; simply put, He was making lemonade from lemons. In truth, the necessity of the Fall—the lemon itself—was an integral part of God's plan from the beginning. The late Elder Boyd K. Packer, a latter-day Apostle, wrote:

> The plan is not based on chance nor on accident. It is based on purpose, on agency, on choice. It accords with laws which were in force long before the plan was ever laid down. All of it has order; all of it was planned for us.[10]

Mortality, with its many trials and tribulations, was such a challenge that God could not, by His very nature as God, force Adam and Eve into it. They had to choose it for themselves. Campbell wrote: "If God had created Adam and Eve mortal beings, he would have negated His own gift of agency."[11]

Again, the Book of Mormon clarifies this point. The Prophet, Lehi, counseling his son, Jacob, wrote:

> And now, my sons, I speak unto you these things for your profit and learning; for there is a God[12] and he hath created all things, both in the heavens and the earth, and all things that in them are, both things to act and things to be acted upon.
>
> And to bring about his [God's] eternal purposes in the end of man . . . it must needs be that there was an opposition [choice]; even the forbidden fruit in opposition to the tree of life. . . .
>
> Wherefore, the Lord God gave unto man that he should act for himself. Wherefore, man could not act for himself save it should be that he was enticed by the one or the other.
>
> And I, Lehi, according to the things I have read,[13] must needs to suppose that an angel of God . . . had fallen from heaven . . . and had become a devil. . . .
>
> And because he had fallen from heaven, and had become miserable forever, he sought also the misery of all mankind. Wherefore, he said unto Eve, yea, even that old serpent, who is the devil, who is the father of all lies, wherefore he said: Partake of the forbidden fruit, and ye shall not die, but ye shall be as God, knowing good and evil.
>
> And after Adam and Eve had partaken of the forbidden fruit they were driven out of the garden of Eden to till the earth.
>
> And they have brought forth children; yea, even the family of all the earth. . . .
>
> Adam fell that men might be; and men are, that they might have joy. (2 Nephi 2:14–20, 25)

We see through Lehi's teaching that the Fall was part of the Father's plan from the beginning, a point that is not made clear in the Biblical text. We also see that, even though men became subject to toil and women to childbirth, to say nothing of the other trials, losses, and crosses of life, the ultimate goal in life is joy: the immortality and eternal life of man (Moses 1:39). Campbell wrote: "Her [Eve's] act, whatever its nature was formally a transgression but eternally a glorious necessity to open a doorway to eternal life."[14]

Opposition in All Things

As Lehi continued his teaching, he told his son that there must be opposition in all things. There must be sorrow for us to appreciate joy. We must experience pain to appreciate the absence of pain. Illness must exist for us to appreciate wellness. Lehi taught:

> For it must needs be, that there is an opposition in all things. If not so, my firstborn in the wilderness [Jacob], righteousness could not be brought to pass, neither wickedness, neither holiness nor misery, neither good nor bad. Wherefore, all things must needs be a compound in one; wherefore, if it should be one body[15] it must remain as dead, having no life neither death, nor corruption nor incorruption, happiness nor misery, neither sense nor insensibility.
>
> Wherefore, it must needs have been created for a thing of naught; wherefore there would have been no purpose in the end of its creation. Wherefore, this thing must needs destroy the wisdom of God and his eternal purposes, and also the power, and the mercy, and the justice of God.
>
> And if ye shall say there is no law, ye shall also say there is no sin. If ye shall say there is no sin, ye shall also say there is no righteousness. And if there be no righteousness there be no happiness. And if there be no righteousness nor happiness there be no punishment nor misery. And if these things are not there is no God. And if there is no God we are not, neither the earth; for there could have been no creation of things, neither to act nor to be acted upon. Wherefore all things must have vanished away. (2 Nephi 2:11–13)

These verses present a powerful spiritual and philosophical treatise on the purpose of life. It is as if God could not create anything with just one side. In his book *Mere Christianity*, C. S. Lewis plainly taught the if one is to have good, he must also have bad. Otherwise, what is good? What is bad? Both qualities of being must be measured against some outside criteria, what Lewis called the *tertiary quid*.[16] God had to create pain for there to be joy, else how would we know either pain or joy?

The Fallen Angel:
The Ultimate Source of Evil

Many people who reject the very existence of a god do so because, they reason, how could a loving god allow such evil to exist in the world? They claim to find no direct or satisfactory answers in the Bible, so they turn away from the Bible and God. In truth, that philosophy is a strong argument *for* the existence of God and His plan for the salvation and exaltation of mankind. We are blessed to know this because of the Book of Mormon. God *must* allow His children to choose, whether for good or ill, or He would cease to be God and, in the process, destroy the agency of man.

If there is evil in the world (and there is), it does not come from God. It comes from the Adversary. The Apostle John wrote:

"And there was war in heaven: Michael and his angels fought against the dragon; and the dragon fought and his angels,

And prevailed not; neither was their place found any more in heaven.

And the great dragon was cast out, that old serpent, called the Devil, and Satan, which deceiveth the whole world: he was cast out into the earth, and his angels were cast out with him. (Revelation 12:7–9)

In the Book of Mormon, Nephi paraphrases Isaiah on the subject when he wrote:

How art thou fallen from heaven, O Lucifer, son of the morning! Art thou cut down to the ground, which did weaken the nations! (2 Nephi 24:12)

Most Christians believe this war in heaven is yet to come. Modern-day revelation teaches us that war occurred before the world was. Satan and his followers were cast out of heaven forever and were cast into this earth. They will never, eons without end, return to heaven, even for another war. Because Satan is eternally damned, he is miserable, and seeks to make others as miserable as he is. The evil in this world originates with him, but it is brought to fruition through the evils and designs in the hearts of conspiring men and women (see D&C 89). In this sense, the war in heaven is still in progress today. Only the battlefield has changed.

God does not delight in the suffering of His children. As He showed the great patriarch, Enoch, He weeps for them when they choose wickedness over Him (Moses 7:28). He weeps when they must suffer the consequences of their disobedience. He weeps when they hurt one another. Nevertheless, He has given them their agency and will not rob them of that agency, even at the price of sorrow.

A Probationary Time

When I try to think of life on earth without agency, I am drawn to two opposite possible conditions taken from literature. The first is the state of the civilization of the fictional city of Camazotz from the book *A Wrinkle in Time* by Madeline L'Engle. There, the people are forced to do everything to the exact and minute specifications of a master IT. They have no agency and, as a result, no freedom or joy.

The second example comes from H. G. Wells's *The Time Machine*, wherein the Eloi, in a post-apocalyptic civilization, live in a paradisiacal garden state of perpetual innocence. They have no trials nor work to do. Their food and clothing and all necessities of life are provided for them so that they can simply play all day. What they don't realize is that the Morlocks, the other post-apocalyptic survivors, who live underground in their world, are fattening them up for ultimate and cannibalistic slaughter. Their very innocence leads to their destruction. Both conditions are too awful to imagine.

Lehi taught the awful state the world would be in had there not been the Fall:

> And now, behold, if Adam had not transgressed, he would not have fallen but he would have remained in the garden of Eden. And all things which were created must have remained in the same state which they were after they were created; and they must have remained forever, and had no end.
>
> And they would have had no children; wherefore they would have remained in a state of innocence, having no joy, for they knew no misery; doing no good, for they knew no sin.
>
> But behold, all things have been done in the wisdom of [God.] (2 Nephi 2:22–24)

Adam and Eve had to fall for man to have his agency. This life was always designed to be a probationary state, a time of testing and trial, a time of growth. The Fall was a blessing.

Accountability

Dr. Viktor E. Frankl once said that since we have a Statue of Liberty on the east coast, we should also have a Statue of Responsibility on the west coast.[17] The two go hand in hand. While we are free to choose our actions, we are not free to choose the consequences of our actions. All choices have consequences and, sooner or later, an accounting must be made of all we have chosen to do. This life is a time to prepare to meet God. We have agency. We also have accountability as to what we do with our agency. Those who argue that it is their choice to do whatever they want often fail to consider the consequences of their choice, both to themselves and to others.

Amulek, the missionary companion of the Book of Mormon prophet Alma the Younger, taught of the dangers of this one-sided, desire-driven thinking. He pleaded with the people he was teaching:

> Yea, I would that ye would come forth and harden not your hearts any longer; for behold, now is the time and the day of your salvation; and therefore, if ye will repent and harden not your hearts, immediately shall the great plan of redemption be brought about unto you.
>
> For behold, this life is the time for men to prepare to meet God; yea, behold the day of this life is the day for men to perform their labors.
>
> . . . I beseech of you that ye do not procrastinate the day of your repentance until the end; for after this day of life, which is given us to prepare for eternity, behold, if we do not improve our time while in this life, then cometh the night of darkness wherein there can be no labor performed. (Alma 34:31–33)

Lehi taught his son Jacob the same thing. He wrote:

> And the days of the children of men were prolonged, according to the will of God, while in the flesh; wherefore, their state became a state of probation, and their time was lengthened, according to the commandments which the Lord God gave unto the children of men. For he gave commandment that all men must repent. (2 Nephi 2:21)

Since we are accountable for our choices and we have consequences as a result, how does this affect us eternally? The Prophet Alma taught that no unclean thing shall inherit the kingdom of God (Alma 40:26) and the Apostle Paul taught that all have sinned (Romans 5:13). Unless we turn away from our sins (which is what *repent* means), we will experience severe eternal consequences.

When I studied psychology at the university, I learned about something that theorists call *cognitive dissonance.* The theory states that once a person has accepted a certain value system, if his behavior violates that value system in anyway, he experiences an uncomfortable mental state that by its very discomfort requires him to either reject his behavior choice or reject the value.

When we sin, by definition, we have violated the value system under which we live. If we have been taught the gospel of Jesus Christ, then it will be God's value system we violate. Cognitive dissonance in these circumstances is called guilt. If we have not deadened our conscience by ignoring it through repeated sin, we will feel guilty. Guilt is not a comfortable emotion and most of us will do anything to rid ourselves of that feeling. If we continue in guilt long enough, we may begin to feel shame. This is an even more dangerous and uncomfortable feeling because, while guilt is attached to the behavior of the one who sinned, shame is attached to the sinner himself. When that happens, it is less likely that the person will repent because he will see *himself* as being wrong or bad instead of understanding that it is his *behavior* that was wrong, and it is therefore subject to change.

When we experience the cognitive dissonance of having sinned, we have three choices:

1. We can recognize our mistake, turn away from it and repent.
2. We can fail to accept that we made a mistake and question the value system and label it as wrong instead of taking ownership that we, in fact, chose the wrong.
3. We can rationalize and excuse our behavior in dozens, if not hundreds of ways, never accepting any accountability for our wrong choices, never seeing any need of correcting those choices.

The word *repent* is found throughout the New Testament. In the Greek, it means *to change one's mind and heart*. The word *repent* is not found in the Old Testament. However, the concept of repentance is. In Hebrew, the connotation is *turning back to God and turning away from sin*. By whatever name it is called, repentance is of vital importance and necessary to return to live with the Father.

In The Church of Jesus Christ of Latter-day Saints, repentance is the second basic principle of the gospel. We read in the Fourth Article of Faith the following:

> We believe that the first principles and ordinances of the Gospel are: first, Faith in the Lord Jesus Christ; second, Repentance; third, Baptism by immersion for the remission of sins; fourth, Laying on of hands for the gift of the Holy Ghost. (Articles of Faith 1:4)

But, one might say, if, by sinning, we have already disqualified ourselves from entering God's presence, what can be done? No one can literally turn back time and erase a mistake. In other words, we cannot save ourselves. How grateful I am that the Father's plan provides a way that we can be saved from our foolish and often wicked choices: the sacrifice of our Lord and Savior, Jesus Christ. Returning to the Articles of Faith, we read:

> We believe that through the Atonement of Christ, all mankind may be saved, by obedience to the laws and ordinances of the gospel. (Articles of Faith 1:3)

I love that this verse states that, while we are saved by God's grace, we must also do our part by obeying His commandments and taking upon ourselves, by covenant, the necessary ordinances of His gospel.

Grace and Works

Many other Christians think that we as Latter-day Saints do not believe in the concept of grace. This is not the case. We do. Latter-day Saints recognize that there is nothing we can do to save ourselves. We understand that no one can "earn" his way into heaven by a string of good deeds. Salvation is a gift which we did not earn, but which is given freely out of Father's love for us, His children. The Apostle John wrote:

> For God so loved the world, that he gave his only begotten Son, that whosoever believeth in him should not perish but have everlasting life. (John 3:16)

We call that gift of love the *Atonement* and recognize that it is the pre-eminent event in the history of the world. But while it is a gift freely given, for it to have full efficacy in our lives, we have a responsibility to bring our lives into harmony with Christ's will. We will not be judged by a list of what we did, right or wrong, but rather by a summary of who we have become. Jesus taught by both precept and example the life we are supposed to strive to live. When we falter or fall short, His sacrifice is there to lift us back on the path of discipleship again.

Over the centuries, some have taught that the gift of the Atonement, freely given, covers everything (which is true); therefore, they reason, it allows them to be free to do whatever they want to do (which is not true!) This fallacious belief has been around since the days of the early Apostles. The Apostle Paul, writing to the Roman Christians, sought to correct this line of reasoning when he said:

> What shall we say then? Shall we continue in sin, that grace may abound?
> God forbid. How shall we, that are dead to sin, live any longer therein? (Romans 6:1–2)

In other words, for Christ's grace to atone for our sins, we must be striving to be "dead to sin" and to live our lives in harmony with Christ and His teachings.

The prophet Alma the Younger preached this doctrine to the Nephites. He reminded them of the captivity of their fathers, including his father Alma, in the land of the Lamanites and how they were saved from that captivity through their repentance. He wrote:

And now I ask of you, on what conditions are they saved? Yea, what grounds had they to hope for salvation? What is the cause of their being loosed from the bands of death, yea, and also the chains of hell? (Alma 5:10)

Alma went on to explain how this miracle occurred. His father, Alma, had listened to the words of the Prophet Abinadi in the courts of wicked King Noah (see Mosiah 15–17). Alma had believed Abinadi's words and was converted to the Lord. Thereafter, he went about preaching Abinadi's words to all who would listen, and many others were converted as a result to Alma's preaching. The younger Alma, in preaching to his people, reminded them of this story. Most of them knew it, having had parents who were part of the original group. Alma went on:

> And according to his [Alma's father, Alma] faith there was a mighty change wrought in his heart. Behold I say unto you that this is all true.
> And behold, he preached the word unto your fathers, and a mighty change was wrought in their hearts, and they humbled themselves and put their trust in the true and living God. And behold, they were faithful until the end; therefore they were saved. (Alma 5:12–13)

These men and women were save temporally from the bondage to the Lamanites, and spiritually from the bondage of the sin they had experienced living under the wicked King Noah. Then Alma's sermon changed, and he asked his listeners:

> And now behold, I ask of you, my brethren of the church, have ye spiritually been born of God? Have ye received his image in your countenances? Have ye experienced this mighty change in your hearts? (Alma 5:14)

That was the miracle. This mighty change of heart was what the Apostle Paul spoke of in his second epistle to the Corinthians:

> For as much as ye are manifestly declared to be the epistle of Christ ministered by us, written, not with ink, but with the Spirit of the living God; not in tables of stone, but in the fleshy tables of the heart. (2 Corinthians 3:3)

Jeremiah prophesied that the day would come when the house of Israel would have the Lord's covenant, not in the external law written upon parchment, but rather:

> I will put my law in their inward parts and write it in their hearts; and will be their God, and they shall be my people. (Jeremiah 31:33)

This is the mighty change of heart of which Alma spoke. The members of the Church in his day had been weak in their testimonies and beginning to slip away on little things. Alma wanted to bring them back from the brink before they went too far. He asked them to remember the testimonies they had once proclaimed. He concluded his sermon by asking:

> And now behold, I say unto you, my brethren, if ye have experienced a change of heart, and if ye have felt to sing the song of redeeming love, I would ask, can ye feel so now? (Alma 5:26)

Remember, these were Alma's brethren in the Church. They and their fathers and mothers had been baptized unto repentance. When we are baptized, we take upon ourselves the name of Christ, and always strive to keep His commandments so that we might always have the Spirit to guide us.

We do not have to do it alone. Jesus Christ is there. The Lord gave a promise to His people through the Prophet Ezekiel:

> A new heart also will I give you, and a new spirit will I put within you: and I will take away the stony heart out of your flesh, and I will give you an heart of flesh. (Ezekiel 36:26)

As Kurt Vonnegut once said, we are human beings, not human doings. By living God's commandments, and repenting of our sins, we can have that new heart. We can become the person the Savior wants us to be. The Book of Mormon teaches Christ's Atonement, love, and grace throughout that entire process, not once but every day we live. The Prophet Nephi summed up the relationship between grace and works in these words:

> For we know that it is by grace we are saved, after all we can do. (2 Nephi 25:23)

The Three Pillars of Eternity

I began this theme with a quote from Elder Bruce R. McConkie regarding what he called *the Three Pillars of Eternity*: the Creation, the Fall, and the Atonement. In this chapter, I have discussed the first two pillars. In the next chapter, I will look more closely at the third pillar: the infinite Atonement of our Lord and Savior, Jesus Christ.

Notes

1. Bruce R. McConkie, "The Three Pillars of Eternity" (Brigham Young University devotional, February 1981), speeches.byu.edu.

2. Thomas R. Valetta, "Some individuals interpret scriptures to say that the Creation was done in six 24-hour days. Does Abraham's usage of 'time' lead us to understand that the Creation was not confined to six 24-hour days as we know them?" *Ensign*, January 1994.
3. The Greek word translated as *word—logos*—among other things can mean *spirit*. It describes Jehovah, the premortal Jesus Christ, who was a spirit being when He created the heavens and the earth. John is saying here that Jehovah/Jesus was with the Father in the beginning and was also a God Himself.
4. Both Genesis and Moses say, "Let *us* go down," "Let *us* create," "in *our* likeness" (emphasis added). Both the Father, Elohim, and the Son, Jehovah, were present and participated in the creation of mankind.
5. See *The Teachings of David O. McKay*.
6. Beverly Campbell, *Eve and the Choice Made in Eden* (Salt Lake City: Bookcraft, 2003), 70–71.
7. Gregory L. Lantz, "Brain Differences Between Genders," *Psychology Today*, February 27, 2014, https://www.psychologytoday.com/blog/hope-relationships/201402/brain-differences-between-genders.
8. Joseph Fielding Smith, in Conference Report, October 1967, 121.
9. Robert L. Millet, "The Man Adam," *Ensign*, January 1994.
10. Boyd K. Packer, "Things of the Soul," *Ensign*, May 1986, 50.
11. Campbell, *Eve and the Choice Made in Eden*, 44.
12. All references to God in this text refer to Jehovah/Jesus Christ.
13. Lehi sent Nephi and his brothers to obtain a set of brass plates then in the possession of a distant cousin, Laban. These plates contained a history of his family genealogy. They also contained the five books written by Moses, as well as the writings of many of the prophets who lived prior to the fall of Jerusalem to the Babylonians. These records were written many generations closer to the original authors than anything we have in our current Old Testament. These were the things Lehi was reading.
14. Campbell, *Eve and the Choice Made in Eden*, 33.
15. Lehi is referring to the state of Adam in the Garden.
16. A tertium quid is from Latin and means "something of uncertain or unclassifiable nature, related to, but distinct from, two, usually opposite, things" (*Collins Dictionary*, s.v. "tertium quid," https://www.collinsdictionary.com/us/dictionary/english/tertium-quid).
17. Viktor Emil Frankl, *Man's Search for Meaning* (1956), 209–10.

THEME 6

The Atonement:
The Third Pillar of Eternity

And Abraham took the wood of the burnt offering, . . . and laid it upon Isaac his son; and he took the fire in his hand, and a knife; and they went both of them together.

And Isaac spake unto Abraham his father, and said, My father: and he said, Here am I, my son. And he said, Behold the fire and the wood: but where is the lamb for a burnt offering?

And Abraham said, My son, God will *provide himself* a lamb for a burnt offering. (Genesis 22:6–8; emphasis added)

The Lord required Abraham to sacrifice his beloved son Isaac upon the altar. As I discussed in earlier chapters, many in the Christian world overlook the powerful connection between the binding of Isaac and Christ's later Atonement for sin. We know from latter-day revelation that God commanded Adam to offer sacrifices upon an altar in the "similitude of the sacrifice of the Only Begotten of the Father which is full of grace and truth" (Moses 5:7). Because of this covenant of sacrifice, all the Great Patriarchs of the Old Testament offered the sacrifice of a lamb upon an altar of stone. But it was given to Abraham to personally feel the anguish that the Father would feel in offering up His Only Begotten Son for the sins of the world. As mentioned earlier, the Book of Mormon clarifies for us that Abraham knew after the fact that what he was doing was in "similitude of God and His Only Begotten Son" (Jacob 4:5).

What I find interesting about the eighth verse of Genesis 22 is Abraham's response to Isaac's question, "Where is the lamb?" Abraham replied: "God will provide *himself a lamb*." I think there is implicit in these words that God Himself will *be* the Lamb, because on this occasion Abraham found a ram caught in a thicket by his horns, not a lamb. God did not *provide* a lamb for Abraham; God *was* Himself the lamb—the Lamb of God.[1] When an angel of the Lord told Abraham, "I know that thou fearest God, seeing | thou hast not withheld they son, thine only son, from me," Abraham was released from sacrificing his son and Isaac was released from being that sacrifice (Genesis 22:16).

There would be no ram in the thicket when Jesus Christ gave His life in the ultimate sacrifice.

The Third Pillar of Eternity

Just as the Creation and the Fall are the first two pillars of eternity, the Atonement is the third pillar. It is the central focus of God's plan for His children. The Father knew from before the beginning of the world that giving man his agency would result in mankind as a unit, and men and women as individuals, sometimes making wrong choices. By so doing, men would be cut off for all eternity from returning to the Father because no unclean thing can dwell in heaven. Man, by himself, could do nothing to rectify this condition. The Father's plan, therefore, was to provide a Savior who could sacrifice Himself to pay the debt of sin, which He did not owe, because mankind, being fallen, incurred the debt of sin that we could not pay.

The very word *atonement* gives us the meaning of the sacrifice. If you pronounce it *at-onement,* it defines the act by which Jesus Christ offered Himself, the Lamb of God, that we might become *at one* with our Heavenly Father again. The Book of Mormon makes it clear that there is no other way that mankind could be saved other than the blood of Jesus Christ, which was freely given for them (see Mosiah 3:17; Alma 38:9; Helaman 5:9).

The Foreshadowing of the Pascal Lamb

The association between the blood of the Lamb of God and salvation is clearly illustrated in the events of the Passover. In the first chapter of this book, I talked about the house of Israel. One of the huge and defining events in the history of Israel was Israel's miraculous deliverance from bondage in Egypt. You will remember that Moses and his brother Aaron came to the Egyptian pharaoh and told him, in the name of the Lord, that he must set Israel free. Pharaoh repeatedly refused that request and God brought plagues upon Egypt as a sign that God would not be mocked. The plagues began with the Nile River being turned to blood and ended with the death of all the firstborn of Egypt, both men and beasts (see Exodus 7–11).

As the deadline for the tenth plague approached, the Lord differentiated between the Egyptians and the Israelites by an act of faith foreshadowing the Atonement and crucifixion. The people of Israel were told to sacrifice a lamb and use the blood of the lamb to paint the doorposts and lintels of every house in Goshen. By this sign the destroying angels would recognize a covenant home and pass over that home, saving the life of every firstborn in Israel (Exodus 11–12). Only then did Pharaoh allow Israel to leave Egypt.

The Children of Israel remembered this day every year at the Feast of the Passover. Jews today still celebrate the feast every spring. The Passover meal consists of seven symbolic foods, including the pascal lamb and unleavened bread (representing the haste of Israel's departure from Egypt).[2]

Israel was saved by the blood of the lamb. This event was a clear representation of the ultimate sacrifice of the Pascal Lamb, Jesus Christ. In Christ's Atonement, we too are saved by the blood of the Lamb.

Atonement Foreshadowed in the Old Testament

The law of Moses talks about the idea of making an atonement. The theme of the Atonement in ancient Israel was looking forward to the day when the Lord Himself would take upon Himself flesh and atone for the sins of the world. There are sixty-nine references to the word *atonement* in the Old Testament. All involved sacrifice. All looked forward to the ultimate sacrifice of Jesus Christ.

There were three major types of sacrifices outlined in the law of Moses. The first is called sin and trespass offering.

Sin and Trespass Offerings

These offerings were designed to strengthen and mend the relationship between the Lord and the penitent sinner. They brought the sinner back into harmony with Jehovah. When a person was aware that he had sinned and was sincerely sorry for what had been done, the person took a sacrifice to the priest at the temple. This sacrifice could be as small as a dove or as large as a young male calf. Part of the ceremony involved the penitent laying his hands upon the animal to be sacrificed as a way of symbolically transferring his sins to the animal. The priest then killed the animal in a certain specified and relatively humane way and sprinkled its blood upon the altar. The meat was then cooked. It, along with the animal's hide, when appropriate, became the property of the priest. In that way it was truly a sacrifice of giving up something of value on the part of the person who was repenting. It also represented the fact that in atoning for sin, the animal's blood was shed in lieu of the person's own blood (Leviticus 19:22). Jewish scholars point out that as the person observes the animal's blood being spilled, he should acknowledge in his own heart an understanding that without the divine grace of an atoning sacrifice, that blood being spilt would be his.

Burnt Offering

The second type of offering was a burnt offering in which the entire animal, having been ritually slain, was laid upon the altar and completely consumed by the fire until there was nothing left but the smoke. This was the kind of offering Elijah made to demonstrate God's power before the priests of Ba'al and the people of Israel. This offering represented the penitent person's complete surrender of his will to the will of the Lord. The smoke was said to ascend to Jehovah as a token of the person's repentance (Leviticus 1:9). In the Old Testament instructions to Levitical priests, it says:

> The life of the flesh is in the blood: and I have given it to you upon the altar to make an atonement for your souls: for it is the blood that maketh an atonement for the soul. (Leviticus 17:11)

Peace Offering

This offering was made as a way of opening communication between the penitent sinner and the Lord, a temporary lifting of the veil, as it were. It was so named because it was created to provide peace to the soul of the penitent sinner, a foreshadowing of that "peace of God that passeth all understanding" through the Lord Jesus Christ (Philippians 4:7).

In the peace offering, the sacrifice was prepared by the priest in the prescribed manner, but instead of going to the priest only, it was divided among the priest, the Levites, and the supplicant. When the penitent sinner ate the sacrificial meal, it was considered a most sacred meal, just as if he were supping with the Lord. It reopened communication with deity as the penitent shared the peace of this meal with God and with his family.

Yom Kippur—the Day of Atonement

Once a year, the high priest offered a special sin offering. Before slaying the animal, usually a young male calf or bullock, the priest laid his hands upon the calf and transferred all the sins which the Children of Israel had accumulated over the entire year. Yom Kippur is the most sacred of all Jewish holidays, and observant Jews celebrate it to this day.

This holiday is still observed among Jews for a twenty-five-hour period beginning at sundown on the first day. It is considered a Shabbat or Sabbath, a day of solemn rest, in which no work should be done. It is a day of fasting and prayer; included in the fasting are both food and water, a prohibition on bathing, anointing oneself with oil, wearing leather shoes, and sexual relations with a spouse.[3]

There are usually five religious services during the day, including the first, during which the cantor confesses the sins of the community.[4] Yom Kippur comes at the end of the Jewish month of Elul when Jews are supposed to take stock of their lives and ask forgiveness.[5]

All the sacrifices discussed above were to be made with the future Atonement of the Messiah in mind, just as our sacrament today is designed for us to look back on Christ's Atonement and seek His forgiveness for our shortcomings each time we partake. Unfortunately, the ancient people became lackadaisical in their participation of these prescribed sacrifices (just as we are sometimes lackadaisical in our observation of the sacrament). As early as the days of Samuel and Saul, the Children of Israel had made a mockery of these sacred ordinances. In 1 Samuel, we read about King Saul having been commanded by the Lord to destroy everything among the Amalekites, but he disobeyed. Saul not only kept their king alive, he also kept the best of their flocks. Saul decided that he could offer some of those animals in sacrifice and the Lord would forgive his utter disobedience to the words of God's prophet. The Lord spoke to the prophet and told him what Saul had done and Samuel traveled immediately to Mount Carmel. He approached the camp of Saul and said:

> What meaneth then this bleating of the sheep in mine ears, and the lowing of the oxen which I hear?
>
> . . . Thou [didst] not obey the voice of the Lord. . . .
>
> And Saul said unto Samuel, Yea, I have obeyed the voice of the Lord . . . and have brought Agag the king of Amalek, and have utterly destroyed the Amalekites.
>
> But the people took of the spoil, sheep and oxen . . . to sacrifice unto the Lord thy God in Gilgal.
>
> And Samuel said, Hath the Lord as great delight in burnt offerings and sacrifices, as in obeying the voice of the Lord? to obey is better than sacrifice and to hearken than the fat of rams. (1 Samuel 15:14, 19–22)

This was the final indiscretion on Saul's part that cost him his kingdom.

Throughout the centuries, righteous sacrifice was celebrated and lost to apostasy over and over as the Israelites progressed through the pride cycle. While there were shining examples such as the reigns of Jehoshaphat, Hezekiah, and Josiah, there were many dark valleys of apostasy as well. After the Babylonian conquest, when the Jews returned to Judah, the high priest Jeshua (Joshua) offered righteous sacrifice.

As the three centuries between Malachi and Matthew progressed, there was great apostasy in Judah. While there were a few righteous Aaronic priesthood holders, such as John the Baptist and his father Zacharias, the temple leadership were as wicked and conspiratorial as any secret combination in scripture.

Atonement Fulfilled in the New Testament

The Raising of Lazarus and the Triumphal Entry

During the last week of Jesus's mortal life, He was called to come to the home of His dear friends, Lazarus, Mary, and Martha. Lazarus was sick unto death and his sisters begged Jesus to come quickly. He purposely waited three days before going to Bethany. Mary and Martha were, of course, brokenhearted because Lazarus had died and had been placed in his sepulcher. The scriptures tell us that Jesus wept at seeing their tears. But He had stayed away for a purpose. He wanted Lazarus to have three days in his tomb. Jewish tradition had it that after three days, there was no question that the individual was truly dead. This timeframe also foreshadowed Jesus's three days in the tomb. Paul was three days unresponsive after his vision of Jesus Christ. King Lamoni in the Book of Mormon was three days unresponsive after his conversion to Christ, as was Alma the Younger after his encounter with the angel of the Lord. These tokens of three days are important.

Jesus had the men who had gathered to roll the stone away from the sepulcher. He stood in the entrance and called, "Lazarus, come forth" (John 11:43). Lazarus was raised from the dead, a fact that no one who saw it could deny. When Jesus went into Jerusalem the first day of the week, He was greeted by multitudes thronging the way and waving palm branches as He entered city, sitting on a donkey as befitting a king.[6] That, along with the second cleansing of the temple, was all the conspirators needed to plot a way to take His life.

Moving toward the Atonement: The Last Supper

The week following the raising of Lazarus was the week of the Passover Feast. Jesus made plans to celebrate the Feast of the Passover with His Apostles. He sent them into Jerusalem to find an appropriate room for the Seder meal. It was a solemn occasion for the Savior, for He knew that His time was short. He would soon take upon Himself all the sins and sorrows of the world, culminating with giving His very life on the cross.

All the history of mankind led up to this moment. The sacrifice made by Adam. The sacrifice made by Abraham and Isaac. The pascal lamb in Goshen. Every faithful sacrifice made under the Mosaic law. All these blood sacrifices were offered to prepare the people for the Atonement of Jesus Christ. All the sacrifices had involved the shedding of blood for the propitiation of sin to bring sinful man back into harmony with his Creator. The Atonement would remain the same, but after that night, the token of the Atonement would be different: no longer the flesh and blood of lambs, but tokens of Christ's body and blood, a way of demonstrating our remembrance of Him.

The Apostles found an upstairs room in a home in the city and there, in privacy and fellowship, Christ began to celebrate His final Passover on earth.

Jesus took bread and broke it and blessed it. He didn't cut it; He tore it, just as His flesh was about to be torn. He gave it to His eleven Apostles (Judas having already left). He said:

> Take. Eat. This is my body which is broken for you: this do in remembrance of me. (1 Corinthians 11:24)[7]

He then blessed the cup and said:

> This cup is the new testament in my blood: this do ye as oft as ye drink it, in remembrance of me. (1 Corinthians 11:25)

Paul makes it clear that this is a *new* testament, a *new* covenant, with *new* tokens. No longer would Israel prepare symbolically for the coming Atonement through the shedding of blood. Once Jesus's blood was shed, any other blood sacrifice would pale by comparison. The covenant found in the law of Moses was fulfilled in Him. Blood sacrifice was no longer required. The new covenant was designed to focus on the remembrance of His great and ultimate sacrifice.

This new covenant was represented in the ordinance that came to be known as the sacrament of the Lord's Supper or simply the sacrament. Members of the Church were counseled from the beginning to partake of the tokens of His Atonement on a regular basis. Each person who partakes should examine his life to make sure that he is worthy to partake because those who partake of the sacrament unworthily do so to the damnation of their souls (see 1 Corinthians 11:27–29).

The Book of Mormon helps us fully understand that when we partake of the sacrament, we are renewing the very covenant we made at baptism. The prophet Mormon tied the two ordinances together when he wrote (echoing the words of Paul):

See that ye are not baptized unworthily; see that ye partake not of the sacrament of Christ unworthily; but see that ye do all things in worthiness, and do it in the name of Jesus Christ, the Son of the living God; and if ye do this, and endure to the end, ye will in nowise be cast out. (Mormon 9:29)

It was also Mormon who taught us, through the writings of his son Moroni, the sacramental prayers, reminding us of the promises we make at baptism and when we partake of the sacrament.

- We signify that we are partaking in remembrance of Christ's Atonement.
- We covenant to take His name upon ourselves.
- We indicate, by covenant, that we will always remember Him.
- We promise to keep His commandments.

God's part of the covenant is that if we partake worthily, we will always have His Spirit to be with us through the gift of the Holy Ghost (see Moroni 4–5).

The Savior completed the introduction of the sacramental covenant and instructed His Apostles in many sacred things. Then, they went out into the night. As they approached the Mount of Olives, Jesus left eight Apostles to wait and took three—Peter, James, and John—with Him into the Garden of Gethsemane.

The Olive Press

A few years ago, Brigham Young University produced a remarkable PBS series titled *Messiah: Behold, the Lamb of God*. Many experts in the study of ancient scripture participated in a beautiful and thoughtful portrayal of Jesus Christ, from His existence before the world was through His life, teachings, Atonement, death, resurrection, and beyond. Speaking of Christ as the pascal lamb, Gaye Strathrem, associate professor of religion at BYU, spoke to the difference in the way Latter-day Saints view the Atonement as compared to many other Christian Faiths. In those faiths, Christ's mission in Gethsemane was to prepare for the Atonement on the cross. Latter-day Saints, however, see Gethsemane as the focal point for the Atonement, not merely a preparation for it.[8]

This viewpoint is supported in the scriptures themselves. In all three of the synoptic gospels,[9] we read that Jesus began to feel the crushing weight of our sins the moment He stepped into the Garden of Gethsemane. Matthew writes:

[Jesus] began to be sore amazed and very heavy; and saith unto them [Peter, James, and John] My soul is exceeding sorrowful unto death. (Matthew 26:33–34; see also Mark 14:37–38)

Luke, who was a physician, adds a medical observation to Jesus suffering in Gethsemane:

Saying, Father, if thou be willing, remove this cup from me: nevertheless, not my will, but thine be done. . . .
And being in an agony, he prayed more earnestly: and his sweat was as if it were great drops of blood falling down to the ground. (Luke 22:42, 44)

Cecilia Peek, an associate professor of the classics in the School of Humanities at Brigham Young University, has degrees in ancient history and Mediterranean archeology. She has studied both Latin and Greek and is well qualified to speak about the Greek language as it is used in the New Testament. She explains that a single word in Greek, *hos,* is used in this reference to Christ's sweat as it were great drops of blood. According to Dr. Peek, the word *hos* can be used as either an adverb or an adjective. Used one way it means that Christ's sweat was metaphorically *like* blood; used the other way, it means that Christ's sweat *was* blood. By referring to the Bible alone, one cannot know what *hos* means.[10]

Once again, clarification comes from the Book of Mormon. In Mosiah 3, we read the account of King Benjamin's prophetic speech about the Atonement of Jesus Christ. He wrote:

And lo, he [Jesus Christ] shall suffer temptations, and pain of body, hunger, thirst, and fatigue, even more than man can suffer, except it be unto death; for behold, blood cometh from every pore, so great shall be his anguish for the wickedness and abominations of his people. (Mosiah 3:7)

According to the Book of Mormon, Christ would and did bleed from every pore.[11]

Another image of the Atonement in Gethsemane is involved in the meaning of the word *Gethsemane* itself. The Garden of Gethsemane was so named because it was on the Mount of Olives where olive presses were present: the name *Gethsemane* means *olive press.* After the olives have been harvested, they are crushed by huge, rolling stones into a mash in which the individual olive can no longer be recognized. This mash is then placed in baskets and put into the olive press, where it is under so much pressure that it exudes both oil and water. The first liquid the comes out of the press is red and it stains anything it touches like blood.[12] This is a fitting comparison to the pressure of the collective sins and sorrows of the world falling upon the shoulders of a sinless man.

Those who have had the privilege to be in Gethsemane and watch the olive press at work testify that it is a powerful spiritual experience that deepens their testimony of Jesus.[13]

He Went Forward and Fell and Prayed

S. Kent Brown, a professor of ancient scripture at Brigham Young University, is an expert in Near Eastern studies and was the director of the BYU Jerusalem Center for three years. He is fluent in Hebrew, Coptic, and Greek. In the BYU series on the Messiah, he referenced the repetitive nature of the scriptures describing Jesus's falling in prayer. He noted that in the original Greek, the verbs are presented in the imperfect tense in all the synoptic gospels. For example, from Matthew we read:

> And he went a little further, and fell on his face, and prayed. (Matthew 26:39; see also Mark 14:35)

According to Dr. Brown, this should be read: "He went forward and fell and prayed; and went forward and fell and prayed; and went forward and fell and prayed."[14] This shows even more clearly the pressure Jesus was feeling under the weight of our sins. We may not fully understand how He atoned for all the sin and sorrow in the world; we only know, by our faith, that He did.

The Trial

The Atonement begun in Gethsemane continued through Jesus's betrayal, arrest, and trial. Many scholars of both ancient scripture and Jewish law have pronounced Jesus's trial as being illegal on many points.

- Both the arrest and the trial were held at night, which is in clear violation of Mosaic law.
- The Sanhedrin was not able to offer unbiased judgment because it was the leaders of the Sanhedrin (Caiaphas and Annas) who hired Judas Iscariot to betray Jesus (another violation of the law).
- When the court sought witnesses against Jesus, they could find none, so they called upon men willing to provide false witness. Even then, the witnesses contradicted one another. Those who testified falsely should have been prosecuted for perjury (which was against Jewish law), and there is no record that they were.
- Hearsay evidence and purely circumstantial evidence were not allowed under Jewish law, and the bulk of the testimony was hearsay.

- The formal charges against Jesus were not in place before the trial commenced, as was required by law, and were changed during the trial itself, from blasphemy to treason, for saying He was the King of the Jews.[15] This was a clear violation of Jewish law.
- The trial was not held in the courts of the Sanhedrin as required by law, but in the home of Caiaphas, the sitting high priest.
- Jesus was taken first to Annas (who was no longer the high priest and, therefore, had absolutely no jurisdiction) before He was taken to Caiaphas.
- The trial was held on the eve of a Sabbath (prohibited under the law of Moses), as there was no chance of revisiting the evidence the next day.
- The Sanhedrin pronounced that He was worthy of the death penalty, which they had no legal authority to do.

I am not a legal scholar and I'm sure there are other points that an attorney familiar with the law of Moses could bring forth. Suffice it to say that the proceedings against Jesus were illegal under the Jews' own laws and certainly part of an evil conspiracy to have Him killed.

While Jesus was held in captivity, He was mocked and spat upon and beaten. The usual instrument for such a beating was a whip, often with bits of bones implanted in the cords. Three of the four gospels refer to this beating as a scourging, which meant it tore flesh from Jesus's body. The ancient prophet Isaiah foretold such a beating as part of the Atonement when he wrote:

> But he was wounded for our transgressions, he was bruised for our iniquities: the chastisement of our peace was upon him; and with his stripes, we are healed. (Isaiah 53:5)

Was His scourging part of the Atonement? I personally believe that it was.

Trials before Pilate and Herod

The Sanhedrin recognized that they could not put Jesus to death. Only the Romans could do so. Therefore, they changed the charge from blasphemy (a religious charge not acceptable in a Roman court of law) to treason, claiming that He said that He was the King of the Jews and, by thus saying, was committing treason against Caesar. They took Christ before Pilate the next morning. When Pilate realized that Jesus was from Nazareth, he sent him to Herod, who was the Roman governor of that province and who happened to be in Jerusalem for the Passover.

Herod found nothing of which he could accuse Jesus, so he ordered Him whipped again. It was Herod's soldiers who first placed a "royal robe" about His shoulders before sending Him back to Pilate.

Pilate's soldiers also mocked Jesus and braided a crown of the branches of a thorny plant that was thrust upon His head. Then, in a royal purple robe, He was taken back before Pilate. Just as Herod found no fault in Jesus that he could prosecute, neither did Pilate find Him guilty of any crime. He wanted to have Jesus whipped again and then released. He asked those who were crying for His death what evil He had done. But the leaders of the Jews began the shout: "Crucify him!" Pilate then washed his hands, symbolically indicating that he did not want Jesus's blood on his hands (see Matthew 27:23–24).

Pilate had remembered a custom which allowed the court to free one prisoner accused of a capital crime in honor of the Jewish Passover. Pilate offered the crowd a choice: Jesus or a convicted murderer named Barabbas. The crowd, undoubtedly salted with people hand-picked by the leaders of the Jews, shouted to give them Barabbas. When Pilate then asked what they would have him do about Jesus, they shouted again "Crucify him!" I find it interesting that in Hebrew, the name *Barabbas* (*bar abba*) means "son of the father." This man, though guilty of many grave sins, was freed while the real Son of the Father, Jesus Christ, who was without sin, was sent to be executed.

The Crucifixion

It was on Golgotha, the place of the skull, the traditional site of execution, that Jesus was brought to be crucified. It was at this point that most Christians believe that Christ's Atonement for our sins begins. Latter-day Saints believe that it continues here, having begun the night before in the Garden of Gethsemane. Just as we must not overemphasize the cross and ignore the Garden, we must also not emphasize the Garden and overlook the cross. In both places and everywhere in between, Jesus placed Himself between us and the adversary. Satan is our accuser before the Father; Jesus is our advocate. He bought that right with every drop of His blood shed in every step, from Gethsemane to the cross.

The Roman soldiers who were commissioned to execute Jesus, along with two condemned thieves, nailed his feet to the cross with one huge, iron nail. They also nailed his hands, outstretched, to the cross. Fearing that the nails would tear through the palms of His hands, they also drove nails through His wrists. Considering the sheer number of nerves in the hands, wrists, and feet, I cannot even begin to fathom the pain of crucifixion. But, in truth, thousands of people have been put to death by crucifixion in the history of the world. Christ's atoning sacrifice wasn't just the suffering He endured on the cross, but the total of all the suffering He endured through bleeding from every pore in the garden, through multiple scourging that caused His body to bleed everywhere the whips touched, through His agony on the cross. This all constituted His Atonement.

Jesus Christ Purchased Us with His Blood

The scriptures often refer to the Atonement as Christ's propitiation for sin (see accounts in both John and Romans). The word *propitiation* means to appease or to regain favor lost through sin. We could not propitiate for our own sins, so Christ, our advocate, completed that act of propitiation for us.

To draw an analogy often used, imagine our sin as a monetary debt we owed to God. In essence, we borrowed against our own salvation through sin and are now unable to pay that debt back. Jesus came forward and offered to pay our debt for us, which the Father accepted, blotting out our debt from the record. We now owe that debt to Jesus. In a sense, He bought us and paid for us. His terms are extremely lenient, if not always easy. By allowing His payment of our debt to gain efficacy in our lives, we must first have faith in Him. This means we not only *believe in* Him, but we *believe* Him when He promised that He has wiped the slate of our sins clean. We must next repent of those sins we committed and present Him with our broken hearts and contrite spirits. Third, we must enter the sacred covenants of the baptism of water and of the Spirit. Finally, we must endure to the end by staying on the path of His promises and covenants and by repenting immediately when we find ourselves slipping. If we have strayed away from the covenant path, we can always come back through sincere repentance. In a recent press conference, President Russell M. Nelson admonished members of the Church to stay on the covenant path and those who have left it for whatever reason to return.[16]

Balancing Mercy and Justice

Some people have a hard time reconciling Jehovah of the Old Testament with Jesus of the New Testament. They see the former as totally interested in justice while the latter is interested solely in mercy. In truth, they are one in the same God, balancing both justice and mercy. The Old Testament prophets, while condemning Israel for its backsliding and foretelling punishment for her sins, also consistently returned to the theme of drawing Israel back into the fold and blessing her with great blessings in righteousness. Jesus, on the other hand, while being consistently merciful in healing the sick and forgiving the penitent sinner, also rebuked the Pharisees and other hypocrites without mercy, for they not only sinned, they knew they were sinning, all the while pretending to be righteous.

The balance between justice and mercy is presented beautifully in the Book of Mormon. In the words of Amulek (who was preaching the coming of Christ before it actually occurred), we read:

> Christ shall come among the children of men, to take upon him the transgressions of his people, and that he shall atone for the sins of the world. . . .
>
> For it is expedient that an Atonement should be made; for according to the great plan of the Eternal God there must be an Atonement made, or else all mankind must unavoidably perish; yea all are hardened; yea all are fallen and are lost, and must perish except it be through the Atonement . . .
>
> For it is expedient that there should be a great and last sacrifice; yea, not a sacrifice of man, neither of beast . . . but it must be an infinite and eternal sacrifice.
>
> Now there is not any man that can sacrifice his own blood which will atone for the sins of another.[17]
>
> And behold, this is the whole meaning of the law, every whit pointing to that great and last sacrifice [that] . . . will be the Son of God, yea infinite and eternal.
>
> And thus he shall bring salvation to all those who shall believe on his name; this being the intent of this last sacrifice, to bring about the bowels of mercy, which overpowereth justice and bringeth about means unto men that they may have faith unto repentance.
>
> And thus mercy can satisfy the demands of justice, and encircles them in the arms of safety, while he that exercises no faith unto repentance is exposed to the whole law of the demands of justice . . .
>
> Therefore may God grant unto you, my brethren, that ye may begin to exercise your faith unto repentance, that ye begin to call upon his holy name, that he would have mercy upon you:
>
> Yea, cry unto him for mercy, for he is mighty to save. (Alma 34:8–11, 14–17)

These verses are so rich with meaning that it is difficult to know where to start. First, while the law of Moses is just (and the Nephites were living it), Amulek preached that the law would be fulfilled with the coming of the Messiah, Jesus Christ, and there would be no more shedding of blood of beasts or men.[18]

Second, Christ was going to come to fulfill the demands of justice and, through His Atonement, allow for mercy. That this was known by prophets, even before He was born, is amply testified in the Old Testament, but never more clearly than in the Book of Mormon.

Third, all men have fallen and all would be lost if an Atonement were not made. No man can atone for his own sins, much less the sins of anyone else. Only a Savior could do that.

Fourth, everything in the law of Moses (for example, animal blood sacrifice) points toward the coming of a divine Savior. If it were not so, all would be lost.

Fifth, He would meet the demand of justice and provide mercy for those who have faith unto repentance. Without such faith and repentance, men are left to face the demands of justice on their own.

Finally, even those who lived before Jesus's advent on the earth can have faith in His coming, repent of their sins, and call upon the mercy of His Atonement, even before it was made, because it is by nature both infinite and eternal.

The Infinite Nature of the Atonement

The word *infinite* refers to things that are endless, or without beginning or end. When Jesus said He was *Alpha* and *Omega,* the beginning and the end, He was not only referring to His eternal existence but the eternal nature of His Atonement as well.

The phrase *infinite atonement* is not found in the Bible, only in the Book of Mormon. But understanding its infinite nature is important to truly understanding the Atonement and its eternal scope. The prophet Nephi wrote:

> Wherefore, it must needs be an infinite atonement. . . . Wherefore, the first judgment which came upon man must needs have remained to an endless duration. And if so, this flesh must have laid down to rot and to crumble to its mother earth, to rise no more.
>
> O the wisdom of God, his mercy and grace! For behold, if the flesh should rise no more our spirits must become subject to that angel who fell from before the presence of the Eternal God, and became the devil, to rise no more.
>
> And our spirits must have become like unto him, and we become devils, angels to a devil, to be shut out from the presence of our God, and to remain with the father of lies, in misery, like unto himself. . . .
>
> O how great the goodness of our God, who prepareth a way for our escape from the grasp of this awful monster; yea, that monster, death and hell, which I call the death of the body and the death of the spirit. (2 Nephi 9:7–10)[19]

The Lord is both just and merciful. While He cannot accept sin with the least degree of allowance (Alma 45:16), through the infinite nature of His Atonement, He can temper justice with mercy. How unjust and unmerciful He would be if His Atonement only offered propitiation for the sins of those who were born after His sojourn on earth! How grateful we should all be that His Atonement is eternal, from everlasting to everlasting, and that any soul who has ever lived, or who will ever live, can bring his sins under the infinite umbrella of His Atonement. He was "the lamb slain from the foundation of the earth" (Revelation 13:8).

Notes

1. The term Lamb of God is referenced nine times in the Old Testament; twelve times in the New Testament; and forty times in the Book of Mormon.
2. Encyclopedia.com, s.v. "Passover," accessed February 17, 2018. https://www.encyclopedia.com/philosophy-and-religion/judaism/judaism/passover.
3. Tori Avey, "What Is Yom Kippur?" toriavey.com, accessed May 25, 2018, https://toriavey.com/what-is-yom-kippur/#ptg4U4qlHcmpPB9c.99.
4. Ibid.
5. Ibid.
6. Horses were considered war animals; donkeys were considered a much worthier animal, and the kings of united Israel rode to their coronations upon donkeys and not horses. The crowd would have recognized the symbolism immediately and seen in it the fulfillment of messianic prophecy (see Zachariah 9:9).
7. Scholars agree that this is chronologically the first (and most detailed) description of Christ's words in the upper room. While Paul was not present at the Last Supper, he heard accounts from the eleven.
8. Gaye Strathearn in *Messiah: Behold the Lamb of God*, directed by Sterling Van Wagenen (Provo, UT: BYUtv, 2010), https://www.byutv.org/show/71029013-dd12-40b7-920b-628c7949e9c0/messiah-behold-the-lamb-of-god.
9. The synoptic gospels consist of Matthew, Mark, and Luke. They are so called because they provide a synopsis of the life of Jesus Christ. The Gospel of John is organized in a different manner and is not considered synoptic.
10. Cecilia Peek in *Messiah: Behold the Lamb of God*.
11. There is an extremely rare medical condition known as hematidrosis, which causes the capillaries that feed the sweat glands to rupture and the pores to exude blood. It is brought on by extreme mental, physical, and emotional stress. According to Wikipedia, the claim of Christ sweating blood is plausible given that hematidrosis has been seen on rare occasions in people awaiting execution or going into battle in wartime (Wikipedia, s.v. "hematidrosis," last modified May 29, 2018, https://en.wikipedia.org/wiki/Hematidrosis).
12. Cecilia Peek in *Messiah: Behold the Lamb of God*.
13. Ibid.
14. S. Kent Brown in *Messiah: Behold the Lamb of God*.

15. It was, in fact, Pilate who asked, "Are you the King of the Jews?" and Jesus answered, "Thou sayest." See Matthew 27:11.
16. Russell M. Nelson in R. Scott Lloyd, "President Russell M. Nelson Named 17th President of the Church," *Church News*, January 16, 2018, https://www.lds.org/church/news/president-russell-m-nelson-named-17th-president-of-the-church.
17. I think Amulek was referring to the "eye for an eye and tooth for a tooth and life for a life" of the Mosaic law.
18. This is a clear differentiation between the law of Moses and Christ's gospel law, which occurred at the time of His Atonement. This transition, while implicit in the sacrament in the Upper Room, is far less clear in the Bible.
19. Spiritual death means permanent separation from God brought about by sin, for which there is no propitiation made.

THEME 7

The Resurrection

In the previous chapter, I talked about the three pillars of eternity as described by Elder Bruce R. McConkie. Just two weeks before his death, in April 1985, Elder McConkie spoke of the "purifying power of Gethsemane" in the spring general conference of The Church of Jesus Christ of Latter-day Saints. Elder McConkie was a scriptural scholar of great repute, and he had a way of drawing pictures with his words. It is easy to see the Creation, the Fall, and the Atonement as the three pillars of eternity. In his final conference address, he talked about three gardens: the Garden of Eden, the Garden of Gethsemane, and the Garden of the Open Tomb. This is how Elder McConkie described each garden:

> In Eden we will see all things created in a paradisiacal state—without death, without procreation, without probationary experiences. [After the Fall, men experienced both death and procreation. After the Fall] a probationary estate of trial and testing will begin.
>
> Then in Gethsemane we will see the Son of God ransom man from the temporal and spiritual death that came to us because of the Fall.
>
> And finally, before an empty tomb, we will come to know that Christ our Lord has burst the bands of death and stands forever triumphant over the grave.[1]

I have discussed the Garden of Eden with the Creation and the Fall and the Garden of Gethsemane beginning the Atonement. It is now important to discuss the third garden, that of the Resurrection, for the Fall brought both sin *and* death into the world. The Atonement gives man the opportunity to repent and have his sins forgiven. The Resurrection allows man to conquer death.

In this theme, I will discuss the physical nature of the Godhead: one in purpose but separate in substance. I will look at common views of the Godhead that are not in line with New Testament teachings and the antecedent of such false doctrine. I will answer the question: Did Jesus literally take up His body again in the resurrection? I will sample dozens of scriptural witnesses from both the Bible and the Book of Mormon that He did. Even given these testimonies, vast numbers of Christians still believe in a Trinity of one god in three, one who has only a spiritual essence. How did men get so far afield? When did it happen?

The Council at Nicaea

There are few events in the Bible that were documented as thoroughly as the reality of Jesus Christ's physical resurrection, and yet there is such confusion today that the Bible accounts have been turned inside out and rationalized away. Christ's Church of the first three centuries AD was very different from much of Christianity we find in the world today. That confusion began while the original Apostles were still alive, but none were formally codified until the Council at Nicaea in the early fourth century AD.

It began when the Roman Emperor Constantine came to the throne of the Eastern Empire. He wanted to reunite the Roman Empire, and he knew that to do that, he would have to unite the disparate sects within Christianity to create a Universal Christian Church. In the summer of AD 325, he invited the 1800 bishops of the Christian Church throughout the known world to meet in Nicaea (modern-day Iznik, Turkey) for the First Ecumenical Council. Records from the time disagree as to the exact number who attended, but it was somewhere between two and three hundred. They came from almost every corner of the Empire.

The historian Eusebius wrote of Constantine at Nicaea:

Resplendent in purple and gold, Constantine made a ceremonial entrance at the opening of the council, probably in early June, but respectfully seated the bishops ahead of himself.[2]

[He] himself proceeded through the midst of the assembly, like some heavenly messenger of God, clothed in raiment which glittered as it were with rays of light, reflecting the glowing radiance of a purple robe, and adorned with the brilliant splendor of gold and precious stones.[3]

Even though Constantine dressed in his kingly robes, he didn't take his original cadre of servants and soldiers. He showed reverence and respect to the bishops and didn't sit until he got their approval to do so.[4]

Contrast that image with that of a humble Peter guiding the first Church conference in Jerusalem less than three hundred years before.

Comparing the Council at Nicaea to the Jerusalem Conference Described in Acts 11

At the first conference in Jerusalem, Church leaders also met to discuss and present their views, just as they would later do at Nicaea. But the Jerusalem conference was made up of men having priesthood authority; the decisions (regarding the baptism of Gentiles) were made by consensus based on the divine revelation given to Peter, the senior Apostle and earthly head of Christ's Church (Acts 10:9–28). At Nicaea, there was no Peter and no Apostles, so decisions were made by argument and, ultimately, by vote. The views that prevailed were based not on divine authority and revelation but on who had the loudest voice, the deepest purse, and the most powerful political alliances. Remember, only 6 percent of the bishops invited even attended! It was the Council of Nicaea that gave us the concept of the Trinity and the doctrines of the Church that prevail in most of Christianity to this day and which changed the doctrines of New Testament Christianity until they were almost unrecognizable. That original false premise of Nicaea, regarding the nature of the Godhead, led to changed doctrine, covenants, and ordinances.

Changed Doctrine

The most significant change wrought by the Nicene Council was concerning the nature of the Godhead. Jesus, His Apostles, and the early Christian leaders taught that the Godhead was composed of God, the Father; God, the Son (Jesus Christ); and God, the Holy Spirit, who were one in purpose but separate in substance (John 17:21).[5] But due to three hundred years' influence of Judaizers and Greeks (who believed God was immaterial and uncreated and unbegotten),[6] the concept of the Trinity was born. This is one example of a Christian Creed coming out of the Council:

> We worship one God in Trinity, and Trinity in Unity, neither confounding the persons, nor dividing the substance. For there is one person of the Father, another of the Son, and another of the Holy Ghost. But the Godhead of the Father, Son, and Holy Ghost, is all one: The Father is incomprehensible, the Son incomprehensible and the Holy Ghost incomprehensible. There are not three incomprehensibles but one incomprehensible. And yet they are not three Gods but one God.[7]

Not only are they one in substance, according to the few at Nicaea, but they are incomprehensible; we can't really know the members of the Godhead and we aren't *supposed* to really know them, despite the fact that Jesus Himself taught: "And this is life eternal, that they might know Thee, the only true God, and Jesus Christ, whom thou hast sent" (John 17:3).

The final argument at Nicaea centered around one letter of the Greek alphabet, the letter *i*—was Jesus *homoousas or homoousias*—of a *different* or *same* substance of the Father?[8] When I hear about this argument, I cannot help thinking it sounds a little like swallowing a camel while straining on a gnat! (see Matthew 23:24). Not being a scholar of ancient languages myself, I am grateful to be taught by those who are. The Council was hesitant to use the latter description, *homoousias* [of the same substance], because even they recognized it as unscriptural, but Constantine pressed the issue and, in the end, the council agreed to let it stand because it was so ephemeral that every sect could interpret it as they pleased.[9] Contemporary Trinitarian scholars note that "no doctrine of the Trinity in the Nicene sense is present in the New Testament" nor "in [the writings of] the Apostolic Fathers."[10]

The Body of Christ

Despite overwhelming evidence in the New Testament of a literal, physical resurrection and a physical, perfected body, most Christians today believe that Jesus has a body of only spirit. This is a direct result of creating the concept of the Trinity. If God is a personage of spirit without "body, parts, or passions . . . large enough to fill the universe yet small enough to dwell in your heart"[11] and the Father and Jesus are one in substance, then how could Jesus have a body? So, the Council decreed: He has no body.

The original idea that Jesus has only a spirit body largely came from Greek philosophy, which stated that anything physical was impure; hence, a god would never have an impure physical body. Some even went so far as to say that Jesus *never* had a body but was a spiritual manifestation from the beginning. There was no birth in Bethlehem, no death on the cross, and no resurrection on Easter morning. This philosophy, called *Docetism*, was already in vogue during the Apostle John's lifetime as he spoke out against it in his second epistle, written most likely from the Greek city of Ephesus. Most Christians today believe He *had* a body but does not have one now. Somehow and somewhere, He laid it down again, although I've yet to read a clear explanation of where and how that happened, considering overwhelming scriptural and first-century Christian accounts of the literal, physical nature of His Resurrection.

Other changes in doctrine were wrought in the Councils of Constantinople in AD 381; Ephesus in AD 431; and Chalcedon in AD 451. One of the truths governing any philosophical debate is that if you begin on a false premise, your conclusions will be false no matter how well thought out or well argued your position. This is what happened in the Universal Church as decisions on church doctrine fell into place like dominos, built on the nature of Jesus and the Godhead decided at Nicaea.

What Does the Bible Say about the Resurrection?

Luke records an event wherein some of the Apostles and disciples were eating a meal behind closed doors, for they feared the Romans would be looking for them. While they were thus engaged, Jesus suddenly appeared in their midst. They were afraid and feared He was a ghost. Jesus told them not to be afraid, for He was not an apparition. He said:

> Peace be unto you. . . . Why are ye troubled? . . . Behold my hands and my feet, that it is I myself: handle me, and see; for a spirit hath not flesh and bones, as ye see me have. And when he had thus spoken, he shewed them his hands and his feet. . . . Have ye here any meat? And they gave him a piece of broiled fish, and of a honeycomb. And he took it and did eat before them. (Luke 24:36, 38–43)

This is an important point: Jesus Himself said He was not a spirit but a being of flesh and bone. Having a corporeal body and being able to eat was compelling evidence of the literal and physical nature of His Resurrection.

The Bible speaks of another time when Jesus ate. After His first appearance, apparently the brethren weren't sure what to do with themselves. Peter decided to go back to what he had done before his call as an Apostle and that was to "go a fishing" (John 21:3). Six other men went with him. They were on the Sea of Galilee near Tiberius when they saw a man, standing on the shore, beckoning to them. It was far enough away that they didn't recognize Jesus. He called out to them, asking if they had caught any fish. When they answered in the negative, Jesus told them to cast their nets on the right side of the boat. These men had been fishing all night with no luck and weren't confident of a catch, but they did as they were told. The nets soon filled with so many fish that the men couldn't draw them on board because of the weight.

Peter knew at once the stranger on the shore must be Jesus, and he cast off his robe, dove into the water, and swam to him. The others followed in the boat. John writes:

> As soon then as they were come to land, they saw a fire of coals there, and fish laid thereon, and bread.

Jesus saith unto them, Bring the fish which ye have now caught. . . .

Jesus saith unto them, Come and dine. And none of the disciples durst ask him, Who art thou? knowing that it was the Lord.

Jesus then cometh, and taketh bread, and giveth them, and fish likewise. (John 21:9–10,12–13)

This is a beautiful chapter from the Apostle John. After the Apostles ate, Jesus took Peter aside and asked, "Peter, do you love me?" to which Peter replied "Yea, Lord." Again, Jesus asked the question and again Peter answered in the affirmative. The Lord asked a third time and Peter answered. Each time, the Savior gave Peter the admonition to feed His sheep. In a setting reminiscent of Jesus's original calling of Peter, Jesus once again committed the first Apostle to be about the work of the ministry. I believe that Jesus allowed Peter to testify of Him in this manner three times because Peter had denied Him thrice on the eve of Christ's arrest. This is a clear example of the post-resurrection Christ leading His Church through His Apostles. When I testify that Jesus is still leading His church here on earth today, I find a great precedent in Peter.

Matthew describes the events of that Resurrection morning in these words:

In the end of the sabbath, as it began to dawn toward the first day of the week, came Mary Magdalene and the other Mary to see the sepulcher.

And, behold, there was a great earthquake: for the angel of the Lord descended from heaven, and came and rolled back the stone from the door, and sat upon it.

And . . . said unto the women, fear not for I know ye seek Jesus which was crucified.

He is not here, for he is risen. . . .

And as they ran to tell the disciples, behold, Jesus met them saying, All hail. And they came and held him by the feet and worshipped him. (Matthew 28:1–2, 5–6, 9)

The Apostle John reports that he and Peter had gone to the sepulcher that first day of the week, but found the tomb empty, with His burial clothing set aside and the napkin which had covered His head neatly folded. They left and noticed that Mary Magdalene was sitting outside the tomb, weeping.

Mary . . . stooped down and looked into the sepulcher,

And seeth two angels. . . where the body of Jesus had lain.

And they say unto her, Woman, why weepest thou? She saith unto them, Because they have taken away my Lord, and I know not where they have laid him.

And when she had thus said, she turned herself back, and saw Jesus standing, and knew not that it was Jesus.

Jesus saith unto her, Woman why weepest thou? whom seekest thou? She, supposing him to be the gardener, saith unto him, Sir, if thou have borne him hence, tell me where thou hast laid him, and I will take him away.

Jesus saith unto her, Mary. She turned herself, and saith unto him Rabboni; which is to say, Master.

Jesus saith unto her, Touch me not; for I am not yet ascended to my Father; but go to my brethren, and say unto them, I ascend unto my Father, and your Father; to my God and your God. (John 20:11–17)

When Mary Magdalene saw Jesus, she was weeping so much that she didn't recognize Him. But when He tenderly spoke her name, as He had undoubtedly done many times before, she recognized His voice and said, "Master." The King James Version says that He told her to "touch me not," but this translation is inaccurate and gives us an erroneous picture of what really happened. The Greek verb is *hapto,*[12] which means *embrace*, and the verb tense used by John is to *cease doing what you are doing*. In other words, Jesus didn't tell her *not to touch* Him but rather *to cease embracing* Him because He had to ascend to His Father. This makes it apparent that Mary was physically embracing Him, and she had to let Him go, both physically and symbolically, so that He would complete His mission to ascend to the Father.

In my studies, I learned some interesting facts about these two accounts of Jesus with Mary and the other Mary. The translation from the Greek into the King James English doesn't completely—and, in the case of Mary, accurately—portray what happened. When the women were going to tell the disciples that the angel at the tomb had told them that He had risen, Jesus met them on the way. The King James said that they "held him by the feet" but the Greek word used in the text, *krateo,* is much stronger.[13] It connotes that they didn't just hold him, they *seized* Him. I love that picture of a group of women who loved Jesus dearly, falling prostrate at His feet and clinging to Him, as if to never let Him go.

The Apostle Thomas was not present the first time Jesus appeared to the other Apostles and, even though he had spent three years following Christ, he did not believe. He said that, unless he could touch the wounds in Jesus's body, he *would* not believe. The Apostle John wrote of this meeting with Thomas:

And after eight days again his disciples were within, and Thomas with them: then came Jesus, the doors being shut, and stood in the midst, and said Peace be unto you.

Then saith he to Thomas, Reach hither thy finger, and behold my hands; and reach hither thy hand, and thrust it into my side: and be not faithless, but believing.

And Thomas answered and said unto him, My Lord and my God. (John 20:26–28)

The Apostle Paul never knew Jesus during His mortal life, but he came to know him during and following his conversion on the road to Damascus. He later preached that he, too, had seen Jesus, and could testify of Him as the resurrected Christ. When writing to the saints at Corinth, Paul bore testimony of the many who had seen Him:

And that he was seen of Cephas [Peter], then of the twelve: And after that, he was seen of above five hundred brethren at once; . . . After that, he was seen of James;[14] then of all the Apostles. And last of all he was seen of me also. (1 Corinthians 15:5)

A key point to remember is that the resurrected Christ didn't appear to everyone at once. Many of the witnesses saw and talked to Jesus several times. The New Testament tells us that Jesus taught His Apostles for forty days, speaking of those things most important pertaining to the kingdom of God, all that Jesus began both to do and teach, the Apostles who He had chosen:

To whom also he shewed himself alive after his passion by many infallible proofs,[15] being seen of them forty days, speaking of the things pertaining to the kingdom of God. (Acts 1:3)

As Jesus told Thomas:

Jesus saith unto him, Thomas, because thou hast seen me, thou hast believed: blessed are they that have not seen, and yet have believed. (John 20:29)

We who have not seen, do we believe? Do we believe that He took up His body as the word *resurrection* implies?[16] From the scriptures, we learn that our spirits are eternal. They existed before we were born (Jeremiah 1:1). They will continue to exist after we die. When we lay down our physical bodies in death, our spirits don't die but live on. On the day of our resurrection, our spirits will once again reside in our bodies, now perfected.[17] Alma taught that when we rise in the resurrection, our same spirit that we had on earth will possess our resurrected bodies (see Alma 34:34).

One must almost trip over the testimonies of many credible witnesses to dismiss the literal nature of Jesus's Resurrection.

Luke tells us in the Book of Acts that after this forty-day ministry, Jesus ascended into heaven and many witnessed that event.

And when he had spoken these things, while they beheld, he was taken up; and a cloud received him out of their sight. . . .

... [Two men in white clothing said], Ye men of Galilee, why stand ye gazing up into heaven? this same Jesus, which is taken up from you into heaven, shall so come in like manner as ye have seen him go into heaven. (Acts 1:9, 11)

Given these testimonies, it is difficult for me to conceive of the Savior as a personage of spirit with no physical body. Why did the gospel writers go to so much effort to make sure that there were many witnesses to His having a physical body if, in the end, He was just a spirit, ephemeral and incomprehensible? Peter testified boldly of the resurrection. Peter knew that, so long as he was alive, he would do all that he could to testify of Jesus, His crucifixion and resurrection. But he also knew that his days in mortality were going to be short. He taught in his second general epistle to the early saints:

Knowing that shortly I must put off this my tabernacle, even as our Lord Jesus Christ hath shewed me.

... I will endeavour that ye may be able after my decease to have these things in remembrance.

For we have not followed cunningly devised fables, when we made known unto the power and coming of our Lord, Jesus Christ, but were eyewitnesses of his majesty.

For he received from God the Father honour and glory when there came such a voice to him from the excellent glory, This is my beloved Son, in whom I am well pleased.

And this voice which came from heaven we heard, when we were with him in the holy mount. (2 Peter 1:14–18)

The Atonement in the Book of Mormon: This Is My Beloved Son

Whenever God the Father is heard speaking on earth, it has been when He introduced His divine Son. One great example of the Father introducing the Son is found in the Book of Mormon.

As Samuel the Lamanite[18] had foretold, the great destruction at the time of Christ's death had come to pass. Those who were the more righteous of the Nephites were gathered in the city of Bountiful at the temple. They were discussing the events that had occurred in fulfillment of Samuel's prophecy. Suddenly they heard a small voice from heaven that caused their hearts to burn within them. A second time, they heard the voice, a little stronger. By the third time, the voice was strong enough that they could understand what it was saying:

Behold my Beloved Son, in whom I am well pleased, in whom I have glorified my name—hear ye him. (3 Nephi 11:7)

Just as the Father had testified of His Beloved Son at Jesus's baptism, on the Mount of Transfiguration, and following Jesus's resurrection in Jerusalem, so did He testify of His Son to the Nephites in the new world. He would testify in the same way 1820 years later when a young boy went into a grove of trees to ask which church on earth was true (see Joseph Smith—History 1:17).

Another Witness of Jesus Christ

As compelling a witness as the Bible is, it has been so tainted by false traditions that it has become easy to rationalize the testimony of a resurrected and corporeal Christ into contradiction upon contradiction. The Bible has been translated hundreds if not thousands of times over the last twenty centuries, which has allowed such confusion and doubts to creep in. The Book of Mormon, on the other hand, was taken directly from the hands of the last ancient prophet who possessed it and, by the gift and power of God, was translated once. This leaves little, if any, room for error. Some of the most beautiful accounts of the resurrected Christ are found within its pages.

Other Sheep

Prior to His death, Jesus told His Apostles the following:

> Other sheep I have which are not of this fold: them also I must bring and they shall hear my voice; and there shall be one fold, and one shepherd. (John 10:16)

Many have tried to explain this away as Christ referring to the Gentiles, but He did not go to the Gentiles personally; they did not hear His voice directly. He later commissioned His Apostles, particularly Paul, to take His gospel to the gentiles, but He personally went only to the house of Israel.

Who were these other sheep? Where would Jesus find members of the house of Israel who were not of the fold in Jerusalem? Remember, the Ten Tribes were scattered throughout the world and no one alive knows where they are; but God knows. Did He visit them? We have no record of which I am aware, with one exception: the Book of Mormon. Lehi was of the house of Israel. The resurrected Jesus Christ appeared to Lehi's descendants in the new land and taught them just as He had taught in Judea. One of the first things Jesus told them was that they were the other sheep of whom He had spoken (3

Nephi 15:21). He also told them that there were yet other sheep that He would visit. Perhaps one day we will have their records too.

Teachings of the Risen Christ

Jesus came to these other sheep to teach them what He had taught the Jews in the old world. These people were of the house of Israel, through Joseph, and were thus entitled to have instruction of the Lord.[19]

His Resurrected Body

While many people today have been led away from the literal nature of Jesus's resurrection because of the philosophies of men, the Book of Mormon account adds 2,500 witnesses to the hundreds listed in the Bible. The first thing Jesus did was to invite the Nephites to come forward and, like Thomas, touch the wounds in His hands, feet, and side.

> Arise and come forth unto me, that ye may thrust your hands into my side, and also that ye may feel the prints of the nails in my hands and in my feet, that ye may know that I am the God of Israel, and the God of the whole earth, and have been slain for the sins of the world.
>
> And it came to pass that the multitude went forth, and thrust their hands into his side, and did feel the prints of the nails in his hands and in his feet; and this they did do, going forth one by one until they had all gone forth, and did see with their eyes and did feel with their hands, and did know in surety and did bear record, that it was he, of whom it was written by the prophets, that should come. (3 Nephi 11:13–14)

Nephi tells us how many people were present. Even if each took only a few seconds in touching His wounds, Christ and the people must have been there for hours. What a testimony of how He loves all the children of God!

Jesus stayed with the people, teaching them many of the same things He taught His followers in Judea. He called twelve special disciples to serve in a similar capacity to the Twelve Apostles in the old world. He organized His Church. He put to rest many of their contentions, such as those involving baptism, and stated that His doctrine was simple: faith, repentance, baptism by immersion, and baptism by fire and the Holy Ghost.

He taught in dozens of small ways that the Law of Moses had been fulfilled in Him (the Nephites had been living the Law of Moses) and that they must now reach up to a higher law written on the tablets of their hearts.[20]

As Jesus completed His first day with the Nephites, He told them His time was at hand and that He would be returning to His father and would return later. As He looked at the faces of the people in the crowd, He saw that they were weeping. He told them:

> Behold, my bowels are filled with compassion towards you.
>
> Have ye any that are sick among you? Bring them hither . . . and I will heal them. (3 Nephi 17:6–7)

The people brought their sick and disabled and He healed them all.

> And they did all, both they who had been healed and they who were whole, bow down at his feet, and did worship him; and as many as could come for the multitude did kiss his feet, insomuch as they did bathe his feet with their tears. (3 Nephi 17:10)

After what had to be an emotional moment for everyone, Jesus asked them to bring their children that He might bless them. The children encircled Him as the adults knelt around them. Jesus knelt in their midst and prayed to Heavenly Father (3 Nephi 17:11–17). Those who recorded this event said that "eye hath never seen, neither hath the ear heard, before, so great and marvelous things" that they heard Jesus speak to His Father.

He arose from prayer and stood amidst the children and said, "Behold, my joy is full." Then He wept and blessed every little child. After this, He wept again and told the multitude: "Behold, your little ones."

And then something most miraculous occurred. Suddenly the heavens were opened, and a concourse of angels came down and encircled Christ and the children. The children were encircled about as with fire, so great was the glory of Jesus and the angels, and the angels ministered to the children.

The final verse of this story is a final testimony of the reality of the resurrection of Jesus Christ, for the prophet wrote:

> And the multitude did see and hear and bear record; and they know that their record is true for they all of them did see and hear, every man for himself; and they were in number about two thousand and five hundred souls; and they did consist of men, women, and children. (3 Nephi 17:25)

Are we like Thomas, who wouldn't believe because he didn't see, or are we like the Nephites, who opened their ears and eyes to pure testimony, did believe, and then did hear and see?

A Final Testimony: Hand-in-Glove

One of the best lessons on birth, life, death, and resurrection was prepared to help children understand.[21] It involves taking a glove and laying it upon a table. The glove is shaped like a hand, but it cannot move because there is no hand in the glove. This is like a physical body with no spirit to make it alive and functional. If we put on the glove, we can move it around; the hand and the glove move like one. When we come to Earth, it is like putting the glove of our physical body on our spirit body. We cannot see our spirits inside our body just as we cannot see our hand inside the glove, but we know it is there because the glove can now move, wiggle its fingers, and pick up objects off the table.

Because life is a finite mortal experience, one day our physical bodies will become too old, or sick, or injured to continue to live. When we take the glove off the hand and lay it on a table, it is like death. When we die, we lay down our physical lives like the glove on the table. That physical body can no longer function or feel. But the spirit body, like our hand, is still alive! We still exist in spirit form.

Because of Christ's physical resurrection, one day we too will be resurrected. We will once again have our physical bodies, like putting the glove back on the hand. This time our physical body will be infinite instead of finite. It will be perfected and no longer subject to pain, temptation, or death. Then, if we have followed Jesus Christ, we will live again with Him and Heavenly Father.

I love this demonstration because it is so simple a child can understand it. It teaches a profound truth in a simple and concrete manner. It makes the resurrection real.

If you were to ask most people today what kind of body Jesus has right now, they will probably tell you God has a spirit body only, large enough to fill the universe and small enough to fit into your heart.[22] But consider this for a moment: without the Atonement and the Resurrection, Christ's Church is just a philosophy of good values and uplifting stories, but it is *not* Christianity. How can we celebrate each Easter and say *He is Risen!* and then deny Him His risen, perfected, and resurrected body?

I testify that He is risen indeed! The Third Garden is as important in the story of Jesus Christ as are the first two gardens. Without the Fall, we would have no agency and no probationary period to learn, fall, repent, and return. Without the Fall, we would have no need for the Atonement. Without the Atonement, we could never return to live with our Father and our Savior. Without the Resurrection, the Atonement would not be complete.

When the Apostle John saw the living Christ in his great apocalyptic vision, he wrote:

> And when I saw him, I fell at his feet as dead. And he laid his right hand upon me saying unto me, Fear not; for I am the first and the last:

I am he that liveth, and was dead; and behold, I am alive for evermore, Amen; and have the keys of hell and death. (Revelation 1:17–18)

These keys are priesthood keys. Through the infinite Atonement, Jesus Christ opened the gates of hell, which allows us the opportunity to repent and live again with the Father. Through the Resurrection, Christ opened the gates of death which allows us to live *forevermore*. Amen.

Notes

1. Bruce R. McConkie, *The Three Gardens of God*, from "The Purifying Power of Gethsemane," *Ensign*, May 1985, 9–11.
2. As quoted in Warren H. Carroll, *The Building of Christendom* (Front Royal, VA: Christendom College Press, 1987).
3. Eusebius Pamphilius, *The Life of Constantine [Vita Constantini]*.
4. "#109: Council of Nicea," *Christian History Institute*, accessed May 31, 2018, https://christianhistoryinstitute.org/study/module/nicea.
5. Jesus prayed that His Apostles would be *one* as He and the Father are one. He certainly didn't imply that those men become one in substance but, rather, that they become one in purpose.
6. Scott R. Peterson, *Where Have All the Prophets Gone?* (Springville, UT: Cedar Fort Publishing, 2005).
7. From the Athanasian Creed, as quoted in Peterson, *Where Have All the Prophets Gone?*, 143.
8. Daniel C. Peterson in *Messiah: Behold the Lamb of God*, directed by Sterling Van Wagenen (Provo, UT: BYUtv, 2010), https://www.byutv.org/show/71029013-dd12-40b7-920b-628c7949e9c0/messiah-behold-the-lamb-of-god.
9. William G. Rusch, ed., *The Trinitarian Controversy* (Minneapolis, MN: Fortress Press, 1980), 19–20; as quoted in Peterson, *Where Have All the Prophets Gone?*, 158.
10. Rusch, *The Trinitarian Controversy*, 19–20; as quoted in Peterson, *Where Have All the Prophets Gone?*, 154. The Apostolic Fathers are those leaders of the Church in the first century AD who, while they were not Apostles, were undoubtedly bishops who had been ordained to the priesthood by one of the Apostles.
11. From the Nicene Creed.
12. *Messiah: Behold the Lamb of God*.
13. Ibid.
14. It is impossible to tell of which James Paul speaks. James the brother of John would have seen Jesus when the Apostles first saw him. Why single him out for a special experience? James, son of Zebedee, was the first of the Apostles to be martyred. He died not long after the Resurrection. I am guessing that this would be James, the brother of Jesus, and the author of the epistle bearing his name.
15. Hebrew for *signs* and *tokens*.
16. The rising again to life of one who was dead (see *Merriam-Webster Online*, s.v. "resurrection," https://www.merriam-webster.com/dictionary/resurrection).

17. Because mortality is in the blood, resurrected bodies are composed of flesh and bone, but not blood (Leviticus 17:11). Whatever they do have must be more pure and eternal than blood. Therefore, blood was so important in sacrifice, including Jesus's.
18. See Appendix B: Book of Mormon Prophets.
19. See Appendix L for a comparison of the Sermon on the Mount and the Sermon at the Temple in the Book of Mormon to see an example of the doctrine Christ taught this branch of the house of Israel.
20. See Appendix L.
21. Boyd K. Packer, *Teach Ye Diligently* (Salt Lake City: Deseret Book, 1975).
22. From the Nicene Creed.

Full Circle: The Gathering of Israel, the Last Days, and the Second Coming

On the Mount of Olives

It was Sunday morning, October 24, 1841, just before dawn. One of the original Twelve Apostles of the Church of Jesus Christ of Latter-day Saints was just crossing the Brook Kidron, heading toward the Mount of Olives in Jerusalem. When he arrived on the Mount, Elder Orson Hyde knelt at a place he had seen in a vision to offer up a prayer he had been inspired to write, dedicating the land, by the authority of the Melchizedek Priesthood, for the gathering of Israel and the return of the Jews.[1]

We are blessed by the fact that Elder Hyde received the text of his prayer by revelation and that he wrote it down. The prayer is lengthy, so I will cover the basic themes of the dedication:

- He dedicated the land of Palestine for the gathering of the Jews.
- He also consecrated the land for the building up of Jerusalem.
- He spoke of the ultimate construction of a temple in Israel.

I dedicate and consecrate this land unto Thee, for the gathering together of Judah's scattered remnants, according to the predictions of the holy Prophets—for the building up of Jerusalem again after it has been trodden down by the Gentiles so long, and for rearing a Temple in honor of Thy name.[2]

Elder Hyde then prayed to God about His Everlasting Covenant with Abraham, Isaac, and Jacob. He remembered the suffering of the children of the patriarchs and how they were scattered throughout all the earth.

O Thou, Who didst covenant with Abraham, Thy friend, and who didst renew that covenant with Isaac, and confirm the same with Jacob with an oath, that

Thou wouldst not only give them this land for an everlasting inheritance, but that Thou wouldst also remember their seed forever. Abraham, Isaac, and Jacob have long since closed their eyes in death and made the grave their mansion. Their children are scattered and dispersed abroad among the nations of the Gentiles like sheep that have no shepherd, and are still looking forward for the fulfillment of those promises which Thou didst make concerning them.[3]

This Apostle then pled for fertility to return to the land, both plant and animal, and that the Lord would move the people toward Him by taking away their hearts of stone and the clouds in their eyes, thus helping them see clearly, and giving to them hearts of flesh: "I will take away the stony heart out of your flesh, and I will give you an heart of flesh" (Ezekiel 36:26).

He asked, if it were God's "good pleasure to restore the kingdom of Israel" and "raise up Jerusalem as its capital."[4] I find this point to be most interesting, considering recent events. The United States has just recognized Jerusalem as the capital of Israel, rather than Tel Aviv. I believe this to be a literal fulfillment of this prophecy. "Thy good pleasure to restore the kingdom unto Israel—raise up Jerusalem as its capital, and constitute her people a distinct nation and government."[6] Toward the end of the prayer, Elder Hyde asked the Father, in the name of Jesus Christ, to remember all of Zion "with all her Stakes, and with all her assemblies,"[7] as a precursor to gathering all of Israel!

David B. Galbraith, writing for the Church magazines in 1991, said the following:

It is no coincidence that historical annals point to the 1840s as a period of awakening among Jews dispersed throughout the world. Out of this new dawn arose men of influence like Moses Hess, Joseph Salvador, Moses Montefiore, Leo Pinsker, and Theodor Herzl. Having been touched by the spirit of gathering, they began to instill in Jews everywhere the desire to return to their ancient homeland.[8]

Theodor Herzl is generally recognized as the father of the Zionist movement, which became a formal organization in 1897. While that may have been the beginning of Zionism as a political entity, I believe the real beginning of this movement began with a solitary prayer on the Mount of Olives fifty-six years earlier.

The Gathering

The Prophet Joseph Smith taught that the gathering of Israel is doctrine. In the Articles of Faith, he wrote:

We believe in the literal gathering of Israel and in the restoration of the Ten Tribes; that Zion will be built upon the American continent; that Christ will reign personally upon the earth; and that the earth will be renewed and receive its paradisiacal glory. (Articles of Faith 1:10)[9]

There are two parts to the gathering. The first is a spiritual gathering; the second is the physical gathering. Several things have occurred that were foretold and that facilitate the gathering of Israel. The first of these was the coming forth of the Book of Mormon.

In a March 2018 article in the *Ensign*, Elder Quentin L. Cook wrote:

The assault on the Bible and the divinity of Jesus Christ has never been more pronounced in my lifetime than it is today.[10]

The entire premise of this book has been to show how the Book of Mormon upholds crucial Bible themes and serves as Another Testament of Jesus Christ. This wonderful book of scripture has been the means of bringing many souls unto Christ, both Jew and Gentile. This spiritual gathering has, to date, brought close to fifteen million people into the Church of Jesus Christ.

The last great prophet to the Nephites, Moroni, sealed up the records of his people with a description of those records and the purpose of them coming forth in the last days. This text is found in full in the Title Page of the Book of Mormon. I quote here from the final paragraph of Moroni's testimony as to the purpose of the book named after his father, Mormon, its chief editor. Wrote he of the Book of Mormon that it was written for our day, the final dispensation of God's great plan of salvation and exaltation.

[The Book of Mormon] is to show unto the remnant of the house of Israel what great things the Lord hath done for their fathers; and that they may know the covenants of the Lord, that they are not cast off forever—And also to the convincing of the Jew and Gentile that Jesus is the Christ, the Eternal God, manifesting himself unto all nations—And now, if there are faults they are the mistakes of men; wherefore, condemn not the things of God, that ye may be found spotless at the judgment-seat of Christ. (Title page of the Book of Mormon)

Restoring the Power of the Covenants and Ordinances

The restoration of the priesthood and of keys to the priesthood has also had a major impact on the spiritual gathering of Israel. While the record of these proceedings is not found in the Book of Mormon itself, it was in the process of translating the gold plates that Joseph Smith found references to the covenants and ordinances of Israel. When he took his questions to the Lord, he was answered by the coming of the resurrected John, who is called the Baptist, who restored the Aaronic Priesthood by the laying on of hands on May 15, 1829. This event was followed by the restoration of the Melchizedek Priesthood a short time later at the hands of the resurrected ancient Apostles Peter, James, and John.

On April 3, 1836, a remarkable event occurred in Kirtland, Ohio. The Saints had just completed the Kirtland Temple, the first Judeo-Christian temple built since Jesus's day. The temple had recently been dedicated and a Sabbath service was being held. After the Prophet Joseph Smith and his counselor Oliver Cowdery had blessed the tokens of the sacrament, they stepped to the altar of the temple and drew the veil of the temple behind them. In that quiet, holy place there occurred a great visitation of leaders from beyond the spiritual veil. The first to appear was Jesus Christ, who accepted the new temple as His house. Then, in succession, they were visited by the same great prophets who had appeared to Jesus on the Mount of Transfiguration. They came for the same purpose: to restore the vital priesthood keys that they held.

The first to appear was Moses, who conferred upon them the keys to the gathering of Israel in the last days. Moses held those keys as the one who gathered Israel out of bondage in Egypt. Moses did not take the ancient Israelites immediately to their promised land; instead he took them to the foot of Mount Sinai, which was known as the Mountain of the Lord. The tabernacle in the wilderness that Moses was commanded to build was to represent Sinai, and the temples of both Solomon and Herod, together with latter-day temples, are often referred to as "the mountain of the Lord's House" (Isaiah 2:2; Micah 4:1). Just as Moses gathered Israel to the Mountain of the Lord, so, too, will latter-day Israel be gathered to the mountain of the Lord's House.

The next was a prophet identified only as Elias, a title meaning *forerunner*. He restored the keys of the gospel of Abraham, the Abrahamic Covenant.[11] According to Elder Bruce R. McConkie, Israel had been scattered because she had forsaken the Abrahamic Covenant. She must be gathered in these last days to renew that covenant and others once again. Israel is gathered again to be the people of the covenant. In this way, all the world's people may be blessed by Abraham's posterity by their return to the covenant and ordinances of the Lord.

The last to appear was Elijah, who restored the keys to the sealing or binding powers, the ones that Jesus gave to His Apostles when He told them that "whatsoever thou shalt bind on earth shall be bound in heaven," that which

Jesus called "the keys to the kingdom of heaven" (Matthew 16:19). These sealings of families for eternity take place in the mountain of the Lord's House, the temples.[12]

The Gathering as Foretold
in the Old Testament

Dr. Camille Fronk Olson, professor of ancient scripture at Brigham Young University, stated that everything about the gathering goes back to the Abrahamic Covenant wherein Abraham was promised that all the people of the world would be blessed by his posterity.[13] We see that in all the events surrounding the gathering of Israel in the last days.

All of Israel's ancient prophets prophesied that Israel would be scattered but in the last days would be gathered again. None spoke so plainly as the Prophet Ezekiel. Ezekiel was an Aaronic priest taken captive into Babylon. He had seen for himself the utter destruction of Jerusalem and the temple. He knew of the total scattering of the northern tribes, because that was relatively recent history to Ezekiel. He also experienced living in Babylon after the captivity. Here are just a few of his prophecies about the gathering:

> Therefore say, Thus saith the Lord God[14]; I will even gather you from the people, and assemble you out of the countries where ye have been scattered, and I will give you the land of Israel. (Ezekiel 11:17)

> Thus saith the Lord God; When I shall have gathered the house of Israel from the people among whom they are scattered, and shall be sanctified in them in the sight of the heathen, then shall they dwell in their land that I have given to my servant Jacob. (Ezekiel 28:25)

> And I will bring them out from the people, and gather them from the countries, and will bring them to their own land, and feed them upon the mountains of Israel by the rivers, and in all the inhabited places of the country. (Ezekiel 34:13)

> After many days thou shalt be visited; in the latter years thou shalt come into the land that is brought back from the sword, and is gathered out of many people, against the mountains of Israel, which have been always waste: but is brought forth out of the nations, and they shall dwell safely all of them. (Ezekiel 38:8)

There are many people who believe this was all fulfilled when the Jews returned out of Persia by the commission of Cyrus, the King. But a careful reading shows that these are yet to be fulfilled. The prophecies talk about all of

Israel gathering from the lands wherein they had been scattered. That did not happen in the days of Cyrus. It also talks about all of Israel dwelling in safety. If we look at the history of modern-day Israel, we can see that there is no safety.

The Gathering as Foretold in the Book of Mormon

The Nephites knew about the promises made to Abraham, Isaac, and Jacob by the Lord. They also knew about the final destruction of the Northern Kingdom and the later destruction of Judah (Lehi had seen in a vision the destruction of Jerusalem and the temple while they were yet traveling in the wilderness). Most importantly, they knew that God's promises are faithful, and that Israel would, in the last days, be gathered again, preparatory for the Second Coming of the Lord Jesus Christ. Lehi's son Nephi wrote:

> And it shall come to pass that my people, which are of the house of Israel shall be gathered home unto the lands of their possessions; and my word also shall be gathered in one. And I will show unto them that fight against my word and against my people, who are of the house of Israel, that I am God, and that I covenanted with Abraham that I would remember his seed forever. (2 Nephi 29:14)

The reference regarding the gathering to "the lands of their possessions" speaks to the literal, physical gathering. The coming forth of His Word, to gather the people as one, refers to the great spiritual gathering.

When Jesus Christ visited the Nephites after His Resurrection, He also taught them about the gathering:

> And verily, I say unto you, I give unto you a sign, that ye may know the time when these things shall take place—that I shall gather in from their long dispersion, my people, O house of Israel, and shall establish again among them my Zion. (3 Nephi 21:1)

The Gathering as Foretold in the New Testament

The Old Testament prophet Micah wrote: "I will surely assemble, O Jacob, all of thee; I will surely gather the remnant of Israel; I will put them together as the sheep . . . in the midst of their fold" (Micah 2:12). This reference to "sheep . . . in the midst of their fold" reminds me of Jesus's reference to "other sheep . . . which are not of this fold" (John 10:16). I believe this is part of the gathering. The Savior stood on the Mount of Olives, overlooking the city of Jerusalem shortly before His death and mourned for the many times He would have gathered Israelites "as a hen gathers her chicks," but they would not (Luke 13:34). In the Book of Mormon, He repeated the same thing after the great destruction of the Nephites at His crucifixion. In this case, He recalled times when He has gathered them, would have gathered them, and will yet gather them (3 Nephi 10:4–6). All of this must happen before the earth is ready for Christ to come again.

Nephi, son of Lehi, wrote the words of the Lord spoken to him regarding the conditions of the world in the last days, when the Book of Mormon and the Bible would be under attack.

> Thou fool, that shall say: a Bible, we have got a Bible, and we need no more Bible. Have ye obtained a Bible save it were by the Jews?
>
> Know ye not that there are more nations than one? Know ye not that I, the Lord your God, have created all men . . . and I bring forth my word unto the children of men. . . .
>
> Know ye not that the testimony of two nations is a witness unto you that I am God, that I remember one nation like unto another. . . .
>
> Wherefore, because ye have a Bible ye need not suppose that it contains all my words; neither need ye suppose that I have not caused more to be written. . . .
>
> For behold, I shall speak unto the Jews and they shall write it; and I shall speak unto the Nephites and they shall write it; and I shall also speak unto the other tribes of the house of Israel, which I have led away, and they shall write it; and I shall also speak unto all nations of the earth and they shall write it.
>
> And it shall come to pass that the Jews shall have the words of the Nephites, and the Nephites shall have the words of the Jews; and the Nephites and the Jews shall have the words of the lost tribes of Israel; and the lost tribes of Israel shall have the words of the Nephites and the Jews. (2 Nephi 29:6–8, 10, 12–13)

The Book of Mormon had to come forth before the gathering could be accomplished in order that the Jews, and all the world, would have the words of the Nephites.[15] It was that day which Ezekiel saw, when the two *sticks* of Judah and Ephraim come together as one in God's hand (see Ezekiel 37:5–10).

Gathering the Gatherers
in the Last Days

The Church of Jesus Christ of Latter-day Saints was formally organized on April 6, 1830. The doctrine of the gathering of Israel was taught from the beginning. New converts felt that they had been hand-picked from the world to rebuild Zion. In the beginning, while their numbers were small, they gathered physically: first to New York, then Ohio, Missouri, Illinois, and finally the Salt Lake Valley. Today, Latter-day Saints are gathered to the stakes[16] of Zion in their own home nations; as Nephi said, *unto the land of their possessions.* It was during the presidency of President Spencer W. Kimball that Saints around the world were told that their land of inheritance was the land in which they then lived. Temples now dot the earth (another sign of the gathering). The primary focus of the gathering in these last days is the preaching of the gospel of Jesus Christ to spiritually gather Israel (and to the Gentiles "grafted" into the olive tree, which represents Israel) to Jesus Christ. Because the Book of Mormon does support the Bible, the two books are powerful in the hands of thousands of missionaries who go out into the world every day to preach Jesus Christ.

President Russell M. Nelson wrote: "Why is this promise of the gathering so crucial: Because the gathering of Israel is necessary to prepare the world for the Second Coming!"[17]

Those who were gathered to The Church of Jesus Christ of Latter-day Saints were sent out almost immediately to preach the restored gospel of Jesus Christ to the world. With the calling of the first missionaries in the fall of 1830, the great work of the gathering began, and it continues to this day. The first wave of missionary work brought in the gatherers, primarily from the British Isles and the Scandinavian countries. Those early members, and later their progeny, would become the gatherers for others, just as the Savior called his Apostles to be "fishers of men" (Matthew 4:19).

Signs of the Second Coming

Volumes have been written about the signs that will precede Christ's coming. People have poured over the books of Daniel, Matthew (chapter 24), and Revelation for centuries, often putting modern interpretations on the symbolic language used by these prophets. I am not going to do so. To even begin to approach such interpretations would be beyond my abilities and the scope of this work. What I will do is refer in generalities to what sometimes are called the signs of the times, with an occasional quote to clarify those generalities.

The Book of Daniel

The main vision of Daniel is in his inspired interpretation of King Nebuchadnezzar's dream. As you will recall, the king had a disturbing dream that he could not understand.

Look then at the dream revealed to Daniel by the power of God:

> Thou, O king, sawest, and behold a great image. This great image, whose brightness was excellent, stood before thee; and the form thereof was terrible.
>
> This image's head was of fine gold, his breast and his arms of silver, his belly and his thighs of brass,
>
> His legs of iron, his feet part of iron and part of clay.
>
> Thou sawest till that a stone was cut without hands, which smote the image upon his feet that were of iron and clay, and brake them to pieces. (Daniel 2:31–34)

Daniel went on to tell the king that the great image he saw represented the kingdoms of the earth, beginning with Babylon and ending with scattered kingdoms, some weak and some stronger. In the days of those kings, God would set up His kingdom as a stone, growing ever larger, until it fills the whole earth (see Daniel 2:44). Latter-day Saints believe that is happening in these last days with the rolling forth of the gathering.

Matthew 24: The Olivet Sermon

Just prior to His death, Jesus called His Apostles together on the Mount of Olives. They had questions about the fate of Jerusalem and the Second Coming of Jesus Christ. This sermon is recorded in all three synoptic gospels, with the Gospel of Matthew being the most in-depth reporting of the sermon. The thing that makes this sermon difficult to understand is that people confuse the prophecy of what would happen in Jerusalem after Jesus's death with what will happen at the end of days.

Joseph Smith had just such questions and he took them before the Lord in prayer. He was instructed to retranslate those passages that, through years of subsequent translations, had become unclear as to which verses refer to Jerusalem and which to the last days. This translation of Matthew 24, known in the Church as Joseph Smith—Matthew, is included in the Church's standard works as part of the Pearl of Great Price. The main difference between this and the Matthew version involves placing the verses in a slightly different order, so the description of the two events are more clearly delineated.

The first twenty verses describe the signs that would occur before the destruction of Jerusalem by the Romans. One of the main signs was to be the "abomination of desolation."[18] Matthew described Jesus's words thus:

> When ye therefore shall see the abomination of desolation, spoken of by Daniel the prophet, stand in holy place, (whoso readeth, let him understand:). (Matthew 24:15)

At that time, the followers of Jesus Christ were to drop literally everything and flee into prearranged places of safety, away from the city of Jerusalem. This event occurred in AD 70 when the Roman General Titus besieged and conquered Jerusalem. Jewish historian Flavius Josephus wrote that more than a million people were killed in Jerusalem because the siege occurred during Passover week, when the city was full of pilgrims. Many devout Christians escaped this fate because they heeded the words of the Savior, fled Jerusalem, and scattered themselves among Christian congregations around the Mediterranean Ocean.

The remainder of the sermon, found in verses 21–51 of the Joseph Smith Translation of Matthew 24, talks about the signs of the times in the days just prior to Christ's second coming. Here are a few signs he mentioned:

False Christs and False Prophets

Elder Bruce R. McConkie wrote: "A false Christ is not a person. It is a false system of worship, a false church, a false cult that says: 'Lo, here is salvation; here is the doctrine of Christ. Come and believe thus and so, and ye shall be saved.'"[19]

The Gathering of Israel

Jesus told his Apostles in Jerusalem that many will say in secret, "I am the Christ," but for them not to be deceived, because the Second Coming shall be as lightning in the east viewed all the way to the west, and everyone shall see it (Joseph Smith—Matthew 1:26). He went on to say that the gathering will be one sign that His coming is near.[20]

The Gospel Will be Preached to All the World

Dr. Richard Draper, emeritus professor of ancient scripture at Brigham Young University, is widely considered among Biblical scholars to be an expert on the apocalyptic books of the Bible. He stated, regarding this point, that Jesus didn't say there would be *conversions* in all the world; only that the gospel would be preached *with significant force.*[21] In that way, the people of the world won't be able to say, "You didn't warn us."

Wars and Rumors of Wars

One only need watch the news to see such wars and rumors of wars on an almost daily basis. The Prophet Joseph Smith prophesied:

> Thus saith the Lord concerning the wars that will shortly come to pass, beginning at the rebellion of South Carolina. (D&C 87:1, referencing the Civil War almost thirty years before it began)

And again:

> At the commencement of the difficulties which will cause much bloodshed previous to the coming of the Son of Man will [begin] in South Carolina. (D&C 130:12, referencing the Civil War before it began)

The first of these prophecies was recorded in 1832. The American Civil War began in 1861, almost thirty years later, with South Carolina seceding from the United States. There have always been wars throughout the history of mankind, but the Civil War ushered in a time of warfare and tension—rumors of war—that will continue until the coming of Jesus Christ.

Iniquity Shall Abound and the Love of Men Shall Wax Cold, as in the Days of Noah

In the words of Elder Neil A. Maxwell:

> As in the days of Noah, people will also be preoccupied with the cares and pleasures of the world. Ironically, most therefore will even miss such signs as God gives pertaining to Jesus' glorious second coming.[22]

The days of Noah were filled with violence and corruption (Genesis 6:11). Elder Maxwell wrote, on another occasion:

> The people of Noah's time were desensitized to real dangers. So we may become in our time. Noah and those with him had to let go of their world or perish with it![23]

What a cautionary tale for us!

John's Great Apocalypse:
The Book of Revelation

As mentioned earlier, an in-depth study of the Book of Revelation is far beyond the scope of this study. I love a quote that Dr. Draper often shared in his various speaking engagements on the study of the book: that the Book of Revelation either finds a man mad or leaves him mad! I made a deep study of the Book of Revelation several years ago for my blog,[24] and while it didn't find or leave me mad, it did take weeks of prayerful and intensive study, sometimes covering only two or three verses in a day. In lieu of that, I'd like to lean on Dr. Draper again for his wisdom and expertise on the topic.[25]

He stated in a roundtable discussion of the New Testament for BYUtv[26] that there are several main themes played out in John's Apocalypse. These include the following:

- The Restoration of the Gospel and the Gathering of Israel
- Malignant Wickedness and Gross Immorality
- Escalating Warfare[27]

Charles Dickens wrote in *A Tale of Two Cities:* "It was the best of times and the worst of times." That sums up the days in which we live. The Book of Mormon was translated and published for the world. The Church of Jesus Christ of Latter-day Saints was restored. Great missionary efforts are going on throughout the world. The nation of Israel was restored in 1948. Great strides in technology have made learning, research, medicine, and almost every aspect of the human condition better. Family history work[28] is growing at an astonishing rate, both within the Church and without, with generations being linked at the click of a cursor. In that respect, this is the best of times.

On the other hand, while good is growing and Israel is gathering, the world seems to be sliding deeper and deeper into immorality, violence, and hatred. The gulf between the righteous and the unrighteous is widening by the day. What makes this condition even more heart wrenching, is the fact that many of those who are most involved in this *malignant wickedness*, truly believe their view of the world is correct! This is the time spoken of by Isaiah where good is called evil and evil is called good, and woe unto any who fall into this trap (see Isaiah 5:20).

What Dr. Draper calls *conspicuous consumption* has run amok in the world. While we have the worldwide financial wherewithal to lessen the gap between the haves and the have-nots, it seems that things are going in the opposite direction, as that gap widens. Men, women, government, banks, large corporations, and other tainted entities seem to think they can buy the world and they do. Meanwhile, much of the world is starving.

These, then, are also the worst of times. As the Church grows, so does the work of the adversary. John the Revelator called this condition *Babylon,* after the ancient empire New Babylon, and he called it the "whore that sitteth upon many waters" (Revelation 17:1).[29] While I don't want to discuss most of the symbols found in Revelation, I would like to share one image which paints a visceral picture of our society in these last days.

> I saw a woman sit upon a scarlet colored beast, full of names of blasphemy. . . .
>
> And the woman was arrayed in purple and scarlet colour, and decked with gold and precious stones and pearls, having a golden cup in her hand full of abominations and filthiness of her fornication:
>
> And upon her forehead was a name written, Mystery,[30] Babylon the Great, the mother of harlots and abominations of the earth. (Revelation 17:3–5)

If we sit with the images for just a moment, we can see, feel, and almost smell and taste the awful state of our world today. God implores us to "come out of Babylon."

Contrast the image of Babylon as a harlot with the image of the righteous at His coming. The righteous are portrayed as being clothed in white garments signifying purity and righteousness, like a bride, with Christ as the Bridegroom (see, for example, Revelation 7:9, 21:3).

Armageddon

The final theme mentioned by Dr. Draper is the increase in violence and warfare. This is as relevant as this morning's newscasts. Things will continue to deteriorate until the final battle of good versus evil in the Valley of Megiddo, the feared and anticipated Battle of Armageddon.

Sometimes people avoid discussions of the last days out of fear. These revelations are not given to us to invite fear but to encourage spiritual preparation. In the parable of the wise and foolish virgins (Matthew 25), the young women who failed to fill their lamps with oil were shut out when the bridegroom [Jesus Christ] came. The five who were prepared with extra oil for their lamps were taken in to the wedding feast.

While no man knows the exact day and hour of the Second Coming, those who live close to the Spirit will not be caught unaware. As Paul wrote to the Saints in Thessalonica:

> But ye, brethren, are not in darkness, that that day should overtake you as a thief.

Ye are all the children of light, and the children of the day: we are not of the night nor darkness.

. . . Let us watch and be sober. (1 Thessalonians 5:4–6)

As Dr. Draper observed, "when we know the day or the hour, it will be too late to prepare." Therefore, if we would be like the five wise virgins, we always have the oil of testimony in our lamps in abundance through fasting and prayer, studying the scriptures, keeping our covenants with God, and staying on the gospel path as true disciples of Jesus Christ. The prophet Lehi had a vision of the Tree of Life with a fruit that was desirable above all other fruit, and which represents the love of God, the Savior of mankind (see 1 Nephi 1:11). Many temptations and obstacles stood in the way of anyone desiring to eat from the tree and the only people who made it were those who held fast to a rod of iron that ran along the path to the tree. This rod represents the word of God. If we want to stay on the safe path to reunite with our Savior and our Heavenly Father, we must cling to their words.

Speaking of the coming forth of the Book of Mormon, the prophet, Mormon, wrote about the best of days:

[The Book of Mormon] shall come in a day when it shall be said that miracles are done away; and it shall come even as if one should speak from the dead. (Mormon 8:25)

And no one need say [the records of the Nephites] shall not come, for they surely shall, for the Lord hath spoken it; for out of the earth shall they come, by the hand of the Lord, and none can stay it; it shall come in a day when it shall be said that miracles are done away; and it shall come even as if one should speak for the dead. (Mormon 8:26)

Mormon also saw the worst of days:

And it shall come in a day when the blood of saints shall cry unto the Lord because of secret combinations[31] and the works of darkness.

Yea it shall come in a day when the power of God shall be denied and churches become defiled and lifted up in the pride of their hearts; yea even in a day when leaders of churches and teachers shall rise in the pride of their hearts, even to the envying of them who belong to their churches.

Yea, it shall come in a day when there shall be heard of fires, and tempests, and vapors of smoke in foreign lands;

And there shall also be heard of wars, rumors of wars, and earthquakes in divers places.

Yea, it shall come in a day when there shall be great pollutions upon the face of the earth; there shall be murders, and robbing, and lying, and deceivings, and whoredoms, and all manner of abomination; . . . But wo unto such, for they are in the gall of bitterness and in the bonds of iniquity. (Mormon 8:27–31)

The Morning of the First Resurrection: The Rapture

As the world is caught in this bipolar state of being, the days wind down. Some Christian churches refer to the phrase "the Rapture." The word *rapture* means *caught up,* and it refers to a coming event described by Paul in his letter to the Saints in Thessalonica. These Christians believe that the Rapture will come prior to the tribulations of the last days. However, the Apostle Paul saw the event of the resurrection of the righteous and the gathering of the righteous still alive occur at the same time.

> For the Lord himself shall descend from heaven with a shout, with the voice of the archangel and with the trump of God: and the dead in Christ shall rise first. (1 Thessalonians 4:16)

> Then we which are alive and remain shall be caught up together with them in the clouds, to meet the Lord in the air: and so shall be ever be with the Lord. (1 Thessalonians 4:17)

Latter-day Saints don't refer to a rapture. Through modern day revelation, we call this event "the morning of the first resurrection" (see D&C 76:63–65), the day of Christ's coming, when the graves shall be opened and the righteous dead, as well as the righteous among those living, will be caught up to meet the Savior. This event comes at the very time of Jesus's arrival, not ahead of the tribulations (see 1 Thessalonians 4:16, 17). The righteous will live through the tribulations, as will the wicked, until Christ comes and sets His feet for a final time upon the Mount of Olives and the Mount shall "cleave . . . toward the east and toward the west" (Zachariah 14:4), and Babylon, as described by John, will fall.

When Babylon, "the mother of harlots," is slain, according to John the Revelator, all those who have trafficked in her wickedness and committed whoredoms with her shall mourn at her passing because they can no longer gain riches through her empire. The prophet Helaman in the Book of Mormon tells us that many will also weep for their lost opportunities to repent and choose Jesus Christ over Babylon. Said Helaman:

> O, that I had repented, and had not killed the prophets, and stoned them, and cast them out. . . . O that we had remembered the Lord our God in the day that he gave us our riches, and then they would not have become slippery

that we should lose them; for behold, our riches are gone from us. (Helaman 13:33)

The first time Jesus came to earth, he came humbly as an infant in almost obscure circumstances. The second time He comes, it will be in such a magnificent and conquering way, wearing a cloak of what Neil A. Maxwell called "reminding red attire,"[32] red in remembrance of His blood spilt for us and red for having "trod the winepress" alone.[33] There will be no secret about it. The entire world we will see him. The evil in the world shall be destroyed, the righteous of the world spared, and Satan will be bound for a thousand years (Revelation 20:2).

The Millennial Reign of Jesus Christ

Once Satan is bound and the wickedness upon the earth destroyed, Jesus Christ will usher in His Millennial Reign. This is the grand, paradisiacal time when all the winding up work of the Creation will be completed. Many prophets have described this beautiful, anticipated time. Here are just a few of the many references found in scripture:

Isaiah

The wolf also shall dwell with the lamb, and the leopard shall lie down with the kid; and the calf and the young lion and the fatling together and a little child shall lead them. They shall not hurt nor destroy in all my holy mountain: for the earth shall be full of the knowledge of the Lord, as waters cover the sea. (Isaiah 11:6, 9)

For behold, I create new heavens and a new earth: and the former shall not be remembered, nor come into mind. (Isaiah 65:17)

The whole earth is at rest and is quiet: they break forth into singing. (Isaiah 14:7)

The wilderness and the solitary place shall be glad for them; and the desert shall rejoice, and blossom as the rose. (Isaiah 35:1–2)

Because Satan will be bound, the earth shall regain its glory as the Garden of Eden before the serpent arrived on the scene. The curses of *weeds* and *pain* will be lifted.

Nephi, Son of Lehi

For behold . . . the time cometh speedily that Satan shall have no more power over the hearts of the children of men. (1 Nephi 22:15)

John, the Revelator

And I saw an angel come down from heaven,[34] having the key of the bottomless pit and a great chain in his hand. And he laid hold on the dragon, that old serpent, which is the Devil and Satan and bound him a thousand years . . . and set a seal upon him, that he should deceive the nations no more, till the thousand years should be fulfilled: and after that he must be loosed a little season. (Revelation 20:1–3)

The difference between the paradisiacal glory of the millennium and that of Eden is that in Eden, God's plan for His children was just beginning. In the millennial reign of Jesus Christ, God's plan has been realized. People have received both physical bodies and a probationary time wherein they could use their agency to choose Jesus or not. A wise man once said, "If, in the end, you have not chosen Jesus Christ it will not matter what you have chosen instead,"[35] God's work and His glory shall then have been completed.

The Full Circle in Summary

I began this book by reading from the Prophet Zachariah about the coming together of the sticks of Judah and Joseph and the two becoming one in God's hand. This is even more than a prophecy regarding the two books; it is a bringing together of two houses, two tribes, two nations: the Southern Kingdom of Judah and the Northern Kingdom of Israel. Bringing together the two records brings together Israel, with its covenants and ordinances, and God's holy priesthood. These records combine to support one another in ways that confound false doctrine, which can lead to both individual and group apostasy. We come to understand in these books that life is a time to prepare to meet God. It is a time of learning and growth, of making mistakes and repenting, of choosing God or something else. Together, they teach us that choices have consequences and that "decisions determine destiny."[36] Both books testify plainly of the birth, life, Atonement, death, and resurrection of our Savior Jesus Christ. By adding the testimony of the Book of Mormon to that of the Bible, we can see that God is the same today and always and that He loves all His children. Finally, the books together teach us to be prepared for the final chapters of Earth's history when God once again will insert Himself into history for the winding down of Earth's temporal life, the destruction of the wicked, and the salvation and exaltation of those who have chosen well.

This, then, is the promise made to Israel, Isaac, and Abraham, that through their seed, all the peoples of the earth will be blessed. Because the Book of Mormon supports and even clarifies vital principles found in the Bible, it is the catalyst for the gathering of Israel, preparing the world for the coming of Jesus Christ for the final time, the ushering in of the millennium, and the future exaltation, through the Atonement of Jesus Christ, of the Father's children.

Notes

1. From a letter written by Orson Hyde to Parley Pratt, as found in chapter 26 of volume 4 of the *History of the Church*, and retrieved February 23, 2018, from http://www.nyx .net/~cgibbons/orson_hyde_prayer.html.
2. *History of the Church* 4:456–57.
3. Ibid.
4. Ibid.
5. Ibid.
6. Ibid.
7. Ibid.
8. David B. Galbraith, "Orson Hyde's Mission to the Holy Land," *Ensign*, October 1991.
9. Of note, Latter-day Saints have also been taught that Jerusalem will be rebuilt and a temple built. A New Jerusalem will be built here in America. It too will have a temple. We believe the gathering to be happening right now across the world as millions of people are gathered to Christ. Like the stakes that held up Moses's tabernacle in the wilderness, we have been told to strengthen our stakes (organizing local structures within the Church). As the Church has grown, over 3,300 stakes are now organized throughout the world, with 159 open and operating temples. There are also 23 new temples in various stages of planning as of 2016 (https://ldschurchtemples.org/statistics).
10. Quentin L. Cook, "When Evil Appears Good and Good Appears Evil," *Ensign*, March 2018, 32.
11. From a discussion with Elder Bruce R. McConkie by his son, Joseph McConkie, as quoted in *Discussions on the Old Testament* (2003), https://www.byutv.org/show/8e989562-a610 -427c-ba89-f0e358a7385b/discussions-on-the-old-testament?q=discussion%20on%20 the%20old%20testament.
12. I cannot remember a time when I didn't know about these prophets conferring priesthood keys on Joseph Smith, but as I did research for this chapter, I recognized for the first time how the three keys are connected and how they relate to the gathering. Vicarious work for the dead is part of the spiritual gathering.
13. Camille Fronk Olsen in *Messiah: Behold the Lamb of God*, directed by Sterling Van Wagenen (Provo, UT: BYUTV, 2010), https://www.byutv.org/show/71029013-dd12 -40b7-920b-628c7949e9c0/messiah-behold-the-lamb-of-god.
14. Whenever a prophet begins a statement with the words "thus saith the Lord," anything that follows is pure prophecy.
15. Remember that the Nephites were descendants of Joseph through his sons, Ephraim and Manasseh.
16. A *stake* is a local entity in the organization of the Church.
17. Russell M. Nelson, as quoted in R. Scott Lloyd, "God Wants His Children to Return to Him, Elder Nelson Teaches," *Church News*, January 28, 2014, https://www.lds.org /church/news/god-wants-his-children-to-return-to-him-elder-nelson-teaches.

18. When a pagan would stand in the Holy Temple, which happened in AD 70 when the Romans besieged Jerusalem.

19. Bruce R. McConkie, *The Millennial Messiah: The Second Coming of the Son of Man* (Salt Lake City: Deseret Book, 1982), 47–48.

20. "For wheresoever the carcass is, there will the eagles be gathered together" (Matthew 24:28). Joseph Smith's translation says that this refers to the gathering of God's elect from the four corners of the earth (Joseph Smith—Matthew 1:27). The word *carcass* can refer to *framework*, not necessarily something that is dead.

21. Richard Draper in *Messiah: Behold the Lamb of God.*

22. Neal A. Maxwell, *Sermons Not Spoken* (Salt Lake City: Bookcraft, 1985), 62.

23. Neal A Maxwell, *Wherefore, Ye Must Press Forward* (Salt Lake City: Deseret Book, 1977), 13.

24. www.drkathyscouchthereprise.blogspot.com

25. Richard Draper, *Buckle Up Your Seatbelt! A Commentary on John's Apocalypse* (Brigham Young University New Testament Commentary Conference, May 2013).

26. Richard Draper, *Acts to Revelation: Discussions of the New Testament*, Brigham Young University, Provo, UT, 2008.

27. Ibid.

28. The gathering includes those now living and those who have died without having heard of Jesus Christ of His Church.

29. See also the parable of the wise and foolish virgins in Matthew 23.

30. See Appendix G: Secret Combinations.

31. See Appendix G: Secret Combinations.

32. Neal A. Maxwell, "Overcome . . . Even as I Also Overcame," *Ensign*, May 1987.

33. Ibid.

34. Latter-day Saints believe this angel was Moroni and that the coming forth of the Book of Mormon by his hand is one of the most important signs preceding the Second Coming of Jesus Christ.

35. As quoted in Bruce R. McConkie, "The Caravan Moves On," *Ensign*, November 1984.

36. Thomas S. Monson, "Ponder the Path of Thy Feet," *Ensign*, November 2014.

CONCLUSION

How grateful I am to have been born in a time when the words of both Judah and of Joseph are together upon the earth. I have been blessed to study them for most of my life and humbled to share them with those who choose to read this book.

This is my personal testimony, borne after years of study and research, praying and coaching by the Holy Spirit. I am not seeking to argue any points of doctrine, for contention is not of God. I am just presenting my thoughts, prayerfully and with great humility, as food for thought. If it touches your heart, then I am grateful.

Gold Canyon, Arizona, Spring 2018

APPENDIX A

Understanding References to the Godhead

The first Article of Faith states:

> We believe in God, the Eternal Father, and in His Son, Jesus Christ, and in the Holy Ghost.

The Latter-day Saint idea of the Godhead as three personages, distinct in substance but united in purpose, is at clear odds with the concept of Trinity as understood by many Christians of other sects. Latter-day Saints are often criticized for their non-understanding of the Godhead to the point that many say that we are not Christians. Nothing could be further from the truth.

Addressing the concept of the Trinity, Elder Jeffery R. Holland of the Quorum of the Twelve Apostles wrote:

> Unfortunately, nearly two millennia of Christian history have sown terrible confusion and near-fatal error in this regard. Many evolutions and iterations of religious creeds have greatly distorted the simple clarity of true doctrine, declaring the Father, Son, and Holy Ghost to be abstract, absolute, transcendent, immanent, consubstantial, coeternal, and unknowable; without body, parts, or passions; and dwelling outside space and time.
>
> In such creeds, all three members are separate persons, but they are a single being, the oft-noted "mystery of the trinity." They are three distinct persons, yet not three Gods but one. All three persons are incomprehensible, yet it is one God who is incomprehensible.
>
> We agree with our critics on at least that point—that such a formulation for divinity is incomprehensible. . . .
>
> How are we to trust, love, and worship, to say nothing of striving to be like, One who is incomprehensible and unknowable?[1]

Referencing God

When the word *God* is used in the scriptures, we need to look at the context of the quote to understand to which member of the Godhead it references:

- Heavenly Father can be referenced simply as God, God the Father, or Elohim.

- References to *God* most often refer to God the Son. The Father steps into our mortal world on rare occasions:
  - » In the creation story, God the Son is the Creator of Heaven and Earth. The Father joins His Son in the creation process with the creation of Adam and Eve. The first twenty-five chapters refer to God in the singular. In verse 26, God is spoken of in the plural: "Let us make man in our own image" (Genesis 1:26). This differentiation among Gods is even more clear in Moses 2.
  - » The baptism of Jesus, when the Father's voice was heard saying, "This is my beloved Son" (Matthew 3:46; Mark 9:7; Luke 9: 35).
  - » On the Mount of Transfiguration (Matthew 17:5; 2 Peter 1:17).
  - » At the temple in Bountiful when Jesus visited the Nephites (3 Nephi 11:17).
  - » Introducing His Son to Joseph Smith to usher in this last dispensation (Joseph Smith—History 1:17).

- Jesus Christ can be referenced by many names. Most references to *God* in the Bible refer to Jesus unless expressly noted as the Father.[2]
  - » Jehovah, His name before His birth (*Yahweh*)
  - » Jesus, His name after His birth (*Yeshua* or *Joshua* in Hebrew)
  - » Messiah (Hebrew for *the anointed one*, as a title
  - » Christ (Greek for Messiah or *the anointed one*), as a title
  - » Son of God
  - » Son of Man
  - » The Word (see John 1:1)Lord
  - » LORD[3]
  - » Savior
  - » I AM

- The Holy Ghost or Holy Spirit is usually referenced by one of these two terms. He sometimes, on rare and holy occasions, is represented in the form of a dove. He is, however, a personage of spirit and is not literally the dove (John 1:32; Luke 3:22; Mark 1:10; Matthew 3:16; 1 Nephi 11:27).
  - » Holy Ghost
  - » Holy Spirit

Notes

1. Jeffery R. Holland, "The Godhead," delivered during the seminar for new mission presidents at the Provo Missionary Training Center on June 23, 2013.
2. In John 1, John says: "In the beginning was the Word; and the Word was with God; and the Word was God." The first reference to God in this context refers to the Father; the second reference to God refers to the Son.
3. Whenever we read the word LORD all in capital letters, it always refers to Jesus Christ.

APPENDIX B

Book of Mormon Prophets

Lehi—A prophet to Judah as found in the Book of Mormon. Although not mentioned in the Old Testament itself, Lehi, along with the prophets Zenos and Zenock, prophesied among the Jews prior to the fall of Judah to Babylon in 600 BC. Lehi began his prophetic call in Judah in the days of King Zedekiah. He was a contemporary with the prophet Jeremiah and preached many of the same things, including the fact that Judah and the Temple would be destroyed. The people didn't want to hear that and considered it to be treasonous, so they sought to take his life. He was warned by God to take his family and just the basic provisions necessary to sustain life and flee into the wilderness.

He continued as the prophet and patriarch to his extended family through their many years of travel from Jerusalem to their eventual arrival at a promised land. As he grew older, he gradually turned over the leadership of his family to his fourth son, Nephi. He continued to serve the Lord as a prophet until his death in the new land.

Nephi—Nephi was the fourth of Lehi's six sons. He was a righteous man from his youth who loved and supported his father as a prophet in Judah. This created a lot of jealousy in two of his older brothers, Laman and Lemuel. They did not accept their father as a prophet and were among those in Judah who felt that God's Temple and God's City would never be destroyed. They spent the entire future of their lives murmuring against their father and their younger brother. Laman felt that as the eldest, he should be the leader of the family, but God passed him over in favor of Nephi.

Two things stand out in Nephi's character. The first was his desire to know for himself, firsthand, from God. When Lehi received a vision or a spiritual witness, Nephi took it directly to the Lord in prayer. He not only received a witness that his father's experience was true, but he was often shown the same vision himself and was able to describe it in greater detail. His second admirable character trait was that he consistently loved and obeyed the Lord. When his father asked the sons to return to Jerusalem to obtain family records from a distant relative, the two oldest brothers balked at the quest. Nephi's statement of faith, "I will go and do as the Lord has commanded," is the oft-quoted hallmark of his life. Nephi had one faithful older brother, Sam, who continually supported Nephi, and two faithful younger brothers, Jacob and Joseph, both born in the wilderness.

Jacob—Jacob was Lehi's fifth son and first born in the wilderness. He, like his older brother Nephi, was a righteous man from birth. He and his younger brother, Joseph, stayed close to Nephi and supported him as prophet and leader. When Lehi died, Laman and Lemuel and those who followed them threatened the life of Nephi and his followers. Jacob was one who followed Nephi to the highlands away from the land of first landing and the people they now called Lamanites. Nephi mentored Jacob and called upon him to speak to the people gathered in conference. He gave a mighty speech in the spirit of prophecy. When Nephi died (about 544–421 BC), Jacob became the prophet of the Church and the leader of the people.

Enos, Jarom, and Omni—(Omni is the brief writing of several of Jacob's descendants: Amaron, Chemish, Abinadom, and Amaleki. Each added little to the plates.) These men were all descendants of Jacob and charged with keeping the records of the spiritual history of the Nephites. Enos wrote about his struggle with repentance, how he went into the forest to hunt and knelt to pray all day and all night before receiving a remission of his sins. He later bore powerful testimony of Jesus Christ. Jarom testified that the Nephites obeyed the Law of Moses and looked forward to the coming of Christ.

Abinadi—Abinadi was a Nephite who lived with an offshoot group of Nephites living in the mountains. Their king, Noah, was the Book of Mormon version of a King Ahab of Israel because he led his people into gross wickedness. Abinadi prophesied that the king and his people must repent, or they would be brought into bondage. They sought his life, but he escaped. Noah continued in wickedness. Two years later, Abinadi returned. This time he prophesied that they had postponed their repentance too long; they would go into bondage. King Noah put Abinadi to death by fire. Only one man listened. His name was Alma.

Alma—During the days of Abinadi, King Noah had perverted the true Church in his land and chosen his own "priests," just like Jeroboam, king of Israel, had done. Alma was one of Noah's "priests." He listened to the prophecies of Abinadi and was convicted of his sins and repented. He wrote down Abinadi's powerful testimony, which is found in Mosiah 11–17. Alma left the court of Noah and began sharing Abinadi's message with any who would listen.

He soon had so many followers it was difficult to continue to fly under Noah's radar, so to speak. He took the people who believed him and the fled the city and came to a large body of water that was called the Waters of Mormon. Alma baptized the people there (Mosiah 18:8–10.) After Alma and his people returned to the main body of Nephites, who were by then living in the low-lands in a land called Zarahemla, he continued to serve as the prophet of the Church. The king was a man named Mosiah, who was the son of a very righteous king, Benjamin.

Alma the Younger—Alma had a son named after him, who was referred to in the Book of Mormon as Alma the Younger to distinguish him from his father. He was friends with the king's four sons, and the five of them wreaked havoc in the kingdom as they sought to destroy the Church and led many into sin.

Alma had an experience with an angel similar to Paul's experience on the road to Damascus. You can read about it in Mosiah 27. Alma reached out to Christ in his anguish and was healed and forgiven. He went on to be one of the greatest prophets and writers in the Book of Mormon. He served as chief judge and prophet of the Church. He later resigned his judge's commission to serve full-time as a missionary among the apostate Nephites.

The Sons of Mosiah—Ammon, Aaron, Omner, and Himni were the sons of the king who sought to destroy the Church with Alma, the Younger. They were present at the conversion of Alma and were also converted. All rejected the kingship and spent their lives as missionaries among the Lamanites (Alma 17–27).

Helaman—Helaman was the son of Alma. When Alma knew it was his time to go, he called Helaman to him and gave him the call to be the next prophet. Helaman was an amazing prophet and leader. The sons of Mosiah had been successful in their missions and many Lamanites had converted to Christ. Because they had been a warlike and murderous people, as part of their repentance, they had broken and buried their swords deep in the earth so they wouldn't be tempted to take them up again. Other Lamanites attacked them, killing a thousand men who refused to defend themselves. Many righteous Lamanite children were raised by their widowed mothers. Years later, when the Nephites were forced to defend themselves against Lamanite attacks, the righteous Lamanites were concerned because they couldn't help the Nephites due to the oath they had taken. However, there were many of the young men who had been born after the oath and were therefore not subject to it. They volunteered serve in the Nephite army. Helaman became their leader because of the sacred nature to this event. These young men became known as the Sons of Helaman or the Stripling Warriors because of their youth. Many of these young men were wounded in the war, but because of their righteousness, none were killed. Helaman loved these young men as if they were his sons until his own death, after which his son Helaman became prophet.

The prophet Helaman had three sons: Shiblon, Helaman, and Corianton. Shiblon and Helaman were righteous young men, but Corianton did not live according to what he had been taught. His negative example led many people to disregard the prophetic words of his father. We read in Alma 36–42 about Helaman's counsel to his three sons. Four of those seven chapters are a call for Corianton to repent. Corianton did repent and become an effective missionary, along with his two brothers.

Nephi, Son of Helaman—Helaman had two sons, whom he named Nephi and Lehi after his forefathers. He desired that their names should be a constant reminder of the righteousness of their ancestors. When Helaman died, his eldest son, Nephi, became the chief judge and record keeper. Although he, like his father, fought diligently against the influence of the Gadianton robbers, he became "weary" of the growing sinfulness of the people. He gave up the judgment seat and, with his younger brother, Lehi, set about to do full-time missionary work. Nephi's prophecies can be read in Helaman 7–16.

The Nephites grew even more wicked than the Lamanites (particularly the Lamanite converts). Nephi and Lehi were imprisoned and persecuted and those who chose to stand with them also suffered. The Nephites were on a collision course with destruction.

Nephi, son of Helaman, left the land and his son, also named Nephi, became the Nephite prophet.

Samuel the Lamanite—While Nephi and Lehi were preaching the gospel to the backsliding Nephites, there was another prophet in the land. We don't know much about him other than his name and the fact that he was a Lamanite by birth. He one day showed up at the Nephite capital city and, from high on the city wall, preached repentance and the coming of Jesus Christ.

Samuel: Signs of the Coming of Jesus Christ—The two prophecies best known that were given by the prophet Samuel are concerning the signs that would be given in the new world about the Savior's birth in Bethlehem and His death on Calvary.

Christ's birth was to be signified by a day and a night and a day when there would be no darkness. A new star would also appear in the sky, signifying the arrival of the Messiah and Savior, just as the star heralded His birth in Bethlehem (see Helaman 14: 2–5).

Just as Jesus's birth was signified by total light, His death would be signified by total darkness and great destruction.

- No light for three days from the moment of Jesus's death until His Resurrection. The darkness would be impenetrable to the degree that fires could not even be lit
- Thunder and lightning and earthquakes for many hours after His death
- Cracks in the earth, both above the earth and below it
- Mountains sunk into valleys
- New mountains appearing where once had been flat lands
- Highways broken up
- Cities made desolate

Nephi, Son of Nephi—This Nephi, along with many other more righteous Nephites and Lamanites, lived to see the signs fulfilled. Nephi is also remembered for his poignant appeal to God on the night before the Savior's birth. The Nephites had been given a sign that would signify His birth. As the years went by, the majority of the people thought the time had passed and that no sign had been or would be given. They set up a date when all who believed in the coming Messiah would be put to death. Nephi prayed all day and all night for the lives of the believers.

Then he heard the voice of the Lord saying: "Lift up you head and be of good cheer; for behold, the time is at hand, and on this night shall the sign be given, and on the morrow come I into the world" (3 Nephi 1:13).

For a short while after the sign, many believed what Nephi was preaching, but many others did not. The Gadiantons had grown so powerful that the Nephites and Lamanites joined forces to defeat them.

The people repented and prospered, but shortly became proud and sinful again. The government was destroyed, and the chief judge murdered. The people divided into tribes and, in this atmosphere where there was no rule of law, another anti-Christ, Jacob, led many away.

Nephi was ministered to by angels. Many prophets were stoned to death, including Nephi's brother, whom he raised from the dead.

Disciples of Christ and the Three Nephites—Thirty-three years after the signs of Jesus's birth were seen, the signs of His death came about. The wicked people were destroyed in those catastrophic events. Those who survived these calamities heard the voice of God through the darkness telling them that they were among the more righteous.

Sometime after the destruction, the people had gathered in Bountiful at the temple. They heard another voice from heaven proclaiming, "This is my beloved Son." The resurrected Christ appeared to the Nephites and taught and ministered unto them.

The prophet Nephi was the first called, followed by his brother Timothy (whom he had raised from the dead) and his son, Jonas. The remaining nine were named Mathoni, Mathonihah, Kumen, Kumenonhi, Jeremiah, Shemnon, Jonas (a different Jonas), Zedekiah, and Isaiah.

These men were prophets and they went about teaching the people the things they had learned directly from the Savior. Before Christ left them, three of them asked if they could tarry on Earth until He returned. We don't know which three were chosen. They are known simply as *the Three Nephites*.

Amos, Amos, and Ammaron—What followed was a miracle enjoyed by very few in this life: after Christ's mission to the Nephites (and the Lamanites who were numbered with them), they had complete peace and prosperity for two hundred years! Toward the end of that time, the people again succumbed to pride. This wasn't a gradual slide into wickedness, but a headlong plunge by a people in open rebellion to God. As the prophet wrote: "They did not dwindle in unbelief, but they did willfully rebel against the gospel of Christ" (4 Nephi 1:38).

These people fell into apostasy because they were lifted up in pride, wearing costly clothes and jewels; they oppressed the poor and divided themselves into social classes. They built churches unto themselves for financial gain but denied the Christ. They persecuted the righteous but allowed the Gadiantons and other secret combinations to flourish.

Nephi had died, leaving the Nephite record to his son Amos. When Amos also died, he passed on the records to his son, also named Amos, who passed on the records to his son, Ammaron. The people were so lost in wickedness that the Three Nephites had been taken from their midst. The Spirit prompted Ammaron to hide the records to protect them from the rampant destruction of holy things and righteous people.

Mormon—When Mormon was only ten years old, he was approached by Ammaron, the keeper of the Nephite records. Ammaron had hidden the sacred records in the Hill Shim until the Lord inspired him as to whom he could entrust them. Ammaron saw that Mormon as a sober and quick child. He told him where the records were hidden, but told him to wait until he was twenty-four years old before going to the Hill Shim and taking the plates of Nephi to continue the record.

Mormon edited one thousand years of Nephite history. He was a great prophet in his own right, leading us to the lessons by writing "and thus we see."

He was a large man, and by the time he was sixteen years old, he was leading the armies of the Nephites in their wars against the Lamanites. The Nephites had a history of fighting only defensive warfare to protect themselves, their families, and their freedoms. But by then, the people were as wicked as the Lamanites and began to fight offensive wars of retribution. Mormon resigned his commission and refused to lead them. He knew that if the Nephites were the instigators of warfare, God would not protect them.

In the end, he was forced to resume his leadership, as his people fought for their very existence, and was present at the final battle, where he was wounded and ultimately died. Before dying, he entrusted his son, Moroni, with the Nephite records and sacred items.

Moroni—Mormon named his son Moroni after the great Nephite, Captain Moroni, whom he admired greatly. In fact, Mormon had written of Moroni that if all men were like him, the powers of hell would be shaken forever (Alma 48:17).

Moroni observed, along with his father, the destruction of the Nephites at a hill called Cumorah. He slipped away with the records and wandered for many years, staying away from the Lamanites, who would put to death any Nephite who would not deny the Christ—and Moroni would not deny the Christ.

He had thought to write little himself, but his life was preserved and, therefore, he was able to record many sacred things. He copied personal letters he had received earlier from his father about many of the sacred ordinances of the gospel. Unlike the Biblical epistles, which were regulatory, these letters were very clear and directive. Many of the things we know about the ordinances of baptism, the administration of the sacrament, and doctrinal issues come from Mormon's letters to his son.

Moroni ended his record with a challenge to all who would read the Book of Mormon. He invites all to read prayerfully and then ask God if the record was true. He promises that if one does that with a pure and purposeful heart, the Holy Ghost will testify of the truthfulness of the book, for the Holy Ghost testifies of the truthfulness of all things (Moroni 10:4–5). He buried the records and Nephite memorabilia prior to his death.

Moroni later appeared as a resurrected being to a seventeen-year-old Joseph Smith. It was he who told Joseph what his mission was to be. He showed him the place where the records were hidden, in a stone box in the side of a hill. Every year, Joseph visited the hill to receive more instructions from Moroni. After four years, Moroni gave him the Nephite record, which Joseph translated by the gift and power of God. After the translation was complete, Joseph returned the records to Moroni.

Latter-day Saints believe that Moroni was the angel spoken of by John the Revelator when he wrote of the last days, "And I saw another angel, standing in the midst of heaven, having the everlasting gospel to preach to the nations of the world" (Revelation 14:6).

APPENDIX C

Anti-Christs in the Book of Mormon

Ezra Taft Benson once wrote: "The Book of Mormon brings men to Christ through two basic means. First, it tells in a plain manner of Christ and His gospel . . . Second, the Book of Mormon exposes the enemies of Christ . . . It fortifies the humble followers of Christ against the evil designs, strategies, and doctrines of the devil in our day."[1]

An anti-Christ is defined as anyone of anything that actively opposes Jesus Christ—either openly or secretly. When people talk about the anti-Christ, they are often referring to the servant of the "beast" described in the Book of Revelation who is to come. While this is a common use of the word, in truth, there have been anti-Christs in the world ever since Cain. The scriptures and the pages of history are full of such references.

One thing that makes the pre-advent Jesus more visible in the Book of Mormon is the fact that when Joseph Smith translated the Book of Mormon, he saw any reference to *the Anointed One* as *Jesus Christ* and recorded it as such. Some critics of the Book of Mormon say they have a problem of "too much Christ before Christ." In fact, there is no time that is "before Christ" because Christ was the Creator! The word for *Anointed One* in Hebrew is *Messiah,* and the Old Testament is full of such references. Therefore, the reader must look carefully for the anti-Christs of the Old Testament because the word *Christ* in not used in any context; but you can find anti-Christs in every wicked king in Judah or Israel who led away their people into sin and away from the Lord for their own gain.

The word *Messiah* in Greek is *Christ.* That was Jesus's title in the New Testament because most of the gospels and epistles were written in Greek, which was the scholarly language of the people, even though the Apostles spoke Aramaic and Hebrew.

While translating the Book of Mormon, Joseph read out loud from the plates and a scribe wrote down his words. Joseph saw every reference to a *messiah* or an *anointed one* in the text as *Christ,* because that is how he saw it as he translated. Mormon, who edited one thousand years of Nephite records into what we now know as the Book of Mormon, also used the name of Jesus Christ as he edited because he lived some four hundred years after Jesus's visit to the Nephites. He too would not have written *Messiah* when the Messiah had already come, and Mormon knew who He was. One of the most important missions of the Book of Mormon is "to the convincing of the Jew and the gentile that Jesus is the Christ" (title page of the Book of Mormon).

The Book of Mormon is very clear in its description of several anti-Christs: men like Sherem, Korihor, and Nehor, as well as anti-Christ political philosophies, such as the king men, the Zoramites, and men like Amalakiah. If we carefully read about these men and the things they taught, we can see concepts and philosophies that were present in the scriptural accounts that are just as prevalent today as they were in ancient times. Our anti-Christs today also are leading people astray and away from Jesus Christ. Here are three of the best-known anti-Christs in the Book of Mormon. I am giving a lot of information about each so that you can see the pernicious teaching and techniques they used to lead people astray, because there are many of these types of philosophies in our world today. Theirs is a cautionary tale that, if heeded, can save us a lot of confusion and grief.

Sherem

The first anti-Christs mentioned in the Book of Mormon arose during the administration of the prophet Jacob, Nephi's younger brother. Sherem was very open in declaring that his mission was to lead people away from God and the Church. Jacob wrote that Sherem[2] was a brilliant man and very well educated. He was very charismatic and spoke with such power and flattery that many people listened and believed. He sought audience with Jacob to confront him about the things he, as the prophet, was teaching the people. He hoped to win the debate and further his cause. Here are some of the philosophies that Sherem taught:

- There will be no Christ.
- The prophet, Jacob, wasn't really a prophet because there were no prophets and, thus, he was leading the people astray with his preaching of the gospel and of the coming of a Redeemer, Jesus Christ.
- Any preaching of Jesus perverts the right way of God, which is the law of Moses. We have no need for a Christ because the law will save us.
- Any preaching of Jesus is blasphemy.

- No man can know about things that will happen in the future; therefore, there will be no Christ.
- If Christ should come, I would not deny him; but there is no Christ, nor will there be in the future.

Jacob had faith that could not be shaken. He asked Sherem if he studied and believed the scriptures (from the brass plates Nephi had obtained while in Jerusalem). Jacob then testified that prophecies of the coming of Messiah are found all through the scripture, for "none of the prophets have written . . . save they have spoken concerning this Christ" (Jacob 7:11). He then bore his personal testimony of the divinity and mission of Jesus Christ.

Sherem asked Jacob to give him a sign. Jacob refused lest he tempt God, but he left it up to God to decide. If Sherem received a sign, it would not be because of Jacob but rather because of the will of the Lord.

Immediately, Sherem fell to the ground and was taken to his bed, where he became worse for many days. He, like Saul of Tarsus and Alma the Younger, knew without a doubt who had smitten him. He had asked for a sign and had received one. Finally, as he was near death, he asked for the people to come so that he could recant his false testimony. He then bore his testimony of Jesus Christ and of the Holy Ghost and the ministering of angels. He told everyone who would listen that he had been deceived by the devil and prayed that he had not committed the unpardonable sin. He had lied to God and denied the Christ. When he completed his confession before God and men, he died.

In his writings, Jacob said that the contention that had surrounded Sherem had passed and his people returned to the scriptures. Peace came to the nation of Nephi and the people turned away from the words of Sherem.

This was not the case with the other anti-Christs, as you will see.

Korihor

One of the clearest examples of an anti-Christ is Korihor. His perverted teachings prevailed among the Nephites for generations after his death. The tragic story of Korihor is found in Alma 30. Here are some examples of the false doctrine this anti-Christ taught. You can recognize in Korihor's messages the philosophies of the world today.

- No one knew about coming Messiah / Old Testament prophecies concerning His coming are false.
- There is no Jesus Christ.
- Believing in God/Jesus is foolish.

- No one can predict the future; therefore, beliefs in prophets and prophecies are just foolish traditions.
- The only things a person can know are those things he can see, touch, or hear.[3]
- Believing that Jesus Christ can cleanse you of your sins is insanity.[4]
- There is no sin, therefore there is no need for a remission of sins and no need for a Savior.
- Everything a man gets in this life is by his own effort, intelligence, and strength.[5]
- There is no life after this one, so do whatever you want; it is not a sin; you won't be punished.
- Men are fools if they bind themselves to God by "foolish ordinances."[6]
- Religious leaders only want power: they want to assume authority over people; keep them ignorant; and make them feel bad about themselves just for doing what they want to do.
- People who believe in Jesus Christ and seek to obey His commandments are slaves in bondage.
- It is impossible for one man to die and save everybody from sin.
- Clergy keep people slaves because they make them afraid to do anything they want to do for fear it will get them in trouble with the clergy or offend some unknown being—a god that never has and never will exist.

One of the most pervasive techniques used by this master manipulator is this: Korihor tells the people what they believe and then he tells them why it is wrong! Unfortunately, this is a common practice in our society today, used by those who wish to tear down someone else's faith: they deliberately state things about the belief that are not true and then proceed to knock the belief based on their own lies. Korihor either misstates the belief entirely or he takes the belief out of context and twists it to suit his argument—a true anti-Christ.

Korihor eventually asks for a sign and is struck dumb. He then admits that he always knew there was a God and that the devil had deceived him (therefore it is Satan's fault and not his fault—another argument one hears today). In the end, Korihor is run down in the streets and dies. Mormon adds one of his editorial comments in verse 60 when he says, "And thus we see . . . that the devil will not support his children at the last day."

Nehor

In the first chapter of the Book of Alma, we read about a large and imposing man named Nehor. The last good king of the Nephites, Mosiah, had set up a system of laws with judges to govern. Mosiah had four sons, but all four had chosen to serve missions among the Lamanites and, therefore, there was no successor to the throne. Mosiah's solution was a brilliant one: do away with royalty completely and return to the legal system that God had created among the Children of Israel from their very beginning in their promised land.

One of the laws indicated that a man could not be prosecuted for his beliefs. So many dissenters from the Lord's Church had learned to preach false doctrine from the position that what they were preaching was what they truly believed. They knew that perjury (lying) was a punishable offense. Therefore, even if they didn't really believe what they were saying and were just using it as an easy way to make money, they had to preach *as if* they believed. They would then be protected under the law.

One such a professor of incorrect doctrine was a large and powerful man named Nehor. He preached "what he termed to be the word of God" (Alma 1:3). His major themes were:

- There should be a paid clergy. Priests and teachers should not have to work other jobs, but that they should be supported by the people they taught. By the way, he became very wealthy as he built up a church for his own glory.
- Clergy should be popular. Their celebrity status would be a platform to preach opposing ideas to those that were prevalent, including political ideas such as it was politically correct to bring personal and legal pressure against God's church and its system of judges.
- He taught that all men would be saved in the end for God had created all mankind and would, therefore, automatically redeem all mankind. The result of this was that people were free to do pretty much whatever they wanted, so long as they didn't break a civil law, without fear of judgment or punishment (Alma 1:4). This was a clear perversion of the concept of agency and freedom. It encouraged people to believe that their freedom to choose (which was guaranteed in the law) was also freedom to choose no consequences, a very dangerous philosophy.

Nehor established a church of Nehor that was to plague the Nephites for generations. As a result, he did become very popular because he preached an easy, selfish, and lazy way to salvation. He became very rich and began to dress and act as if he were a celebrity. He became "lifted up in the pride of his heart" (Alma 1:6).

This pride led to the arrogance that no one should openly disagree with him or try to impede his work among the people. The people who believed him—and there were many—fawned around him like sycophants. It became politically correct, to borrow a modern word, to support the philosophies of Nehor and his "church."

One day, as he was preaching among his followers, he ran into an old man who just happened to be in that group of people. This old man, whose name was Gideon, had lived among an apostate group (see Mosiah 19) when he was younger, and he saw the devastation that follows the pride cycle. It was he who helped lead these apostates out of bondage after they had fully repented and turned back to God. He spoke openly against Nehor because he recognized his lies. I can hypothesize that Gideon was bearing fervent testimony, casting serious doubt about Nehor and his teachings. Otherwise, I don't believe that Nehor would have been so angry. In a moment of rage, Nehor drew his sword and hit Gideon repeatedly. Because Gideon was old, he was killed by the blows.

Nehor was brought to trial before the chief Nephite judge, Alma the Younger. Alma pointed out to him that, so long as he kept the civil laws, he had freedom to preach what he *thought* to be true. But as soon as he crossed the line and committed murder, he was subject to a sentence of death. He was taken to the top of a hill where he finally confessed that he knew what he had been teaching was a lie (which was perjury under Nephite law), "and there he suffered an ignominious death" (see Alma 1:15).

At his sentencing, the judge, Alma, pointed out that by Nehor's preaching and actions, he had introduced *priestcraft* among the people. Priestcraft is a serious situation because it is not punishable by law, even though it wreaked havoc amongst the people because it results in divisiveness. In modern times, President Abraham Lincoln said that "a house divided against itself cannot stand" in reference to the divisiveness that ultimately led to the American Civil War. Divisiveness, like that which occurs through priestcraft, turns the people against one another, resulting in great political turmoil that makes the nation vulnerable to domestic violence as well as possible attack from hostile nations. Alma tells Nehor that he has been guilty of introducing priestcraft among the people, but he was being executed not for what he preached, but because he sought to enforce his preaching by violence and murder.

Even though Nehor was dead, the problems with priestcraft, which he initiated among the Nephites, grew exponentially until there were many professing false doctrines. This resulting in chaos amongst the people and the people began to bring lawsuits against one another, which overloaded the courts. This problem was exacerbated by the fact that a significant number of judges began to realize that they could make money from this. While clergy were not paid in God's Church, the civil judges were paid, according to a preset formula, for the hours they spent in judgement. Therefore, these judges "did stir up the people to riotings, and all manner of disturbance and wickedness, that they might have more employ, that they might get money according to the suits which were brought before them. . . . Now, it was for the sole purpose to get gain because they received their wages according to their employ" (Alma 11:20).

Alma, by then, had resigned as chief judge and returned to fulltime missionary work because he realized that his society's problems would require God's intervention. While preaching in a town called Ammonihah, Alma was rejected. He left the city in fear for his life. Nevertheless, the Lord, through an angel bid him return. On his return, he found one good man who was willing to listen to him. This man's name was Amulek. He was so thoroughly converted to the truth that he became Alma's missionary companion.

Zeezrom

Zeezrom qualifies as an anti-Christ, but one who had the opportunity to turn his life around.

On their joint mission, Alma and Amulek were confronted by this very outspoken man. The scriptures describe him as "a man who was expert in the devices of the devil, that he might destroy that which was good" (Alma 11:21). After Amulek had born his testimony to the people, Zeezrom began to question him, not because he wanted clarification, but he wanted to twist Amulek's words into a different context to confuse the people who were listening. Here are some of his questions. A careful reader can immediately spot the direction Zeezrom is trying to lead the people. Because of the wickedness of the judges and the contention they had encouraged, it had become politically correct to challenge those who testified of the existence of God and a Messiah. Zeezrom took full advantage of that political climate.

- First, he tried to bribe Amulek with money to deny the very existence of any Supreme Being. This, Amulek refused to do.[7]
- He twisted the same question by saying "so you say there is a Supreme Being?" This was a ploy to trap Amulek because Amulek had just born testimony that there was a God.
- He asked how Amulek knew all of this and Amulek testified of his personal experience with an angel.
- Zeezrom questioned the coming of any sort of Messiah. He then asked if this Messiah Amulek preached would be the Son of God. Amulek, of course, affirmed that was exactly who He was.

Then things began to get nasty. You can see why Zeezrom qualifies as an anti-Christ; he is slowly misinterpreting Amulek's words and twisting them to imply that there is no Christ.

- Zeezrom asks Amulek if Christ will save the people *in* their sins. Note the word *in*. Amulek answered that the Messiah would not save His people *in* their sins.
- Zeezrom pounced on that and said to the people something to the effect of: "See, even this man admits that the Son of God will come, but He will not save His people." Note the lack of the word *in*, by which device he is leading the people away from Amulek's testimony of the coming of the Anointed One. He asked if the Son of God truly is God. Amulek then bore a beautiful testimony of the divinity of Jesus Christ. In our world today, when people set the Bible at naught, and try to deny the divinity, if not the actual existence, of Jesus Christ, the Book of Mormon is consistent in the testimonies of prophets that Jesus is the Christ, the Son of the Living God.

Zeezrom is unusual in many ways. In the beginning, he was a classic example of an anti-Christ, but when Amulek bore such a powerful testimony of Christ, fear struck Zeezrom as he realized by the testimony of the Holy Spirit that Alma and Amulek were right. In fact, he and the other people who were around him began to tremble because Amulek, through his testimony, had laid bare Zeezrom's lies.

Then Alma confronted Zeezrom and he didn't pull any punches. He told Zeezrom that his very thoughts were known to God. He had not just lied to the people, he had lied to God, and God knew it (Alma 12). His thoughts were evil and purposely deceptive to lead people away from God, and God knew it. He had been purposely subtle and cunning to drive Alma and Amulek from Ammonihah so that he could effectively nullify their testimonies of Jesus Christ, and God knew it. Alma then bore his powerful testimony of repentance, Atonement, and resurrection, and the saving power of Jesus Christ.

Alma also bore testimony of his experience with sin and of being racked by guilt, almost unto death, for his wicked deception when he realized that God knew his heart. Zeezrom was likewise racked with increasing guilt over his lies until he became sick unto death. When other powerful people, including the judge in Ammonihah, turned against Alma and Amulek, they were imprisoned and eventually driven from the city. Zeezrom tried to undo what he had done to no avail, and he too was driven out. He went to the town of Sidom, where he lay near death, racked with the realization of what he had done to the people of Ammonihah and to Alma and Amulek themselves.

Sometime later, the missionary companions found themselves in Sidom where they had more success in the preaching. They set up a branch of the Church in Sidom. When Zeezrom heard that they were in town, he felt encouraged and sent for them. They came immediately. Zeezrom was critically ill, struck with a fever from his guilt. He begged Alma and Amulek to heal him. Alma took the man's outstretched hand and asked if he believed in Jesus Christ and in His redeeming power. Zeezrom affirmed it all. Alma then blessed him with a priesthood blessing and Zeezrom was healed almost immediately. He leapt to his feet with a shout of joy. Alma baptized him and from then on, Zeezrom went about preaching the gospel of Christ. This is one of the very few examples in the scriptures someone who began as an anti-Christ truly repented and became pro-Christ.

Notes

1. Ezra Taft Benson, "The Book of Mormon is the Word of God," *Ensign*, January 1988.
2. Read about Sherem in the seventh chapter of the book of Jacob.
3. Today, this philosophy can be called either the theory of naturalistic empiricism or logical positivism.
4. This reminds me of the Karl Marx quote: "Religion is the opiate of the masses."
5. This philosophy today is known as secular humanism.
6. In our day, even some Christian churches deny the need for ordinances, such as baptism for salvation.
7. All these quotes come from Alma 11.

APPENDIX D

Old Testament Prophets

The Prophets to United Israel

Samuel—His name means *name of god Man.*[1] Samuel was dedicated to God by his mother. He heard the voice of god as a young child serving in the Tabernacle. He was both a judge in Israel and a prophet. He ordained Saul to be the first king of Israel (1095 BC). Saul fell from grace and was replaced by King David of the House of Judah. David was a child when Samuel anointed him (1063 BC). God told Samuel that He doesn't choose based upon outward appearances, but He looks upon the heart.

Nathan—His name means *he has given.* He served as prophet during the reign of King David (1055 BC). Through Nathan, the Lord took David to task over his adulterous affair with Bathsheba and the murder of her husband. Nathan was also the prophet who had to tell David that the Lord would not allow to build the House of the Lord, the Temple in Jerusalem.

Gad—He was a seer and a prophet. He was a friend to David and David sought his advice. He is said to have helped David arrange the music for psalms to be sung in the Temple.

Prophets to the Northern Kingdom of Israel

After the Civil War, God sent prophets to cry repentance to the Northern Kingdom.

Ahija—He prophesied to King Jeroboam about the ill-advised decision to divide the United Kingdom of Israel and take ten of the tribes in the North. He also rebuked the king in the name of the Lord for his wickedness.

Elijah—He is one of the best-known Old Testament prophets. His name means *Jehovah is God.* He was bold in decrying the wickedness of King Ahab and Queen Jezebel. Israel had been in a complete state of apostasy since their first king, Jeroboam, had built a temple for the heathen god, Baal. He took the high places, once altars and places of worship of Jehovah, and turned them into groves for the immoral worship of Astarte, the fertility goddess of Baal. As wicked as Jeroboam was, Ahab was more wicked and his evil wife, Jezebel's name has become synonymous with the epitome of evil. He began prophesying in 953 BC and is best known for sealing the heavens so that it did not rain.

Elisha—His name means *god shall save*. He was a disciple of Elijah and later became a prophet himself after Elijah's translation. He served for over fifty years.

Hosea—He was one of the last prophets to Israel and the only one who left a written record. He foretold the downfall of Israel due to sin, but also preached God's love for His children.

Prophets to the Northern Kingdom of Israel and to Other Lands

Obadiah—His name means *servant of the Lord*. He was a steward in the house of King Ahab and protected other prophets from the wicked Jezebel.

He also prophesied against the Kingdom of Edom for her hostility toward the Kingdom of Judah at a time when Judah was under extreme pressure from outside nations. Obadiah spoke of Edom's ultimate punishment for this hostility (856 BC).

Jonah—Jonah's name is mentioned in 2 Kings as a prophet to Israel. However, Jonah didn't write about his preaching there, but rather of his call to preach in Nineveh (not far from the modern city of Mosel in Iraq.) Nineveh was the capital of the Kingdom of Assyria, perhaps the deadliest enemy ever faced in the Middle East of the day. They broadcast their atrocities widely to create terror and submission in their enemies. I'm sure Jonah had heard these stories, so when God called him to go to Nineveh, he was terrified. He ran away, hoping to get as far as Spain to and away from God. The ship was hit by a huge storm and it seemed as if they were about to sink. Jonah felt that he was the cause of God's anger. He threw himself overboard to protect his shipmates and was swallowed by a great fish. He spent three days in the belly of the fish before the fish spewed him out and he continued his mission. He preached repentance to the people in Nineveh and, much to his surprise, they repented in sackcloth and ashes! Jonah was angry and spent several days outside the city walls pouting. God taught Jonah a lesson on the preciousness of each soul through a gourd vine growing out of the dirt.

The sign of Jonah is mentioned in connection with Jesus's death in that Jesus spent three days in the tomb as Jonah spent three days in the fish.

Prophets to the Southern Kingdom of Judah

Shemaiah—His name means *the Lord heareth.* He is less well known as a prophet because his ministry began at the dividing of the two kingdoms. He sought to convince Rehoboam not to fight against the Northern Kingdom. The Lord assured his prophet that He, the Lord, would take care of punishing Israel.

Joel—There is some controversy surrounding Joel's ministry as to when it happened. The country was experiencing severe drought and Joel admonished them to repent so that the Lord could bless them again. He was one of the prophets who spoke of *burdens,* referring to the heavy punishments to come upon the wicked if they don't repent.

Amos—He was an interesting prophet. He was a shepherd who lived just south of Jerusalem in Judah, yet his message was a warning for Israel. He spoke of the Lord wanting a sacrifice of personal integrity and righteous living. The animal sacrifices being made were a mockery of the Law because they were being used to *buy* righteousness while staying unrighteous. The Lord told Samuel much the same thing in 1 Samuel 15.

Several of these prophets foretold the utter destruction of the people because of their sins, but then offered the hope of a restoration in the end, a glorious millennial reign that will surpass any former glory. Amos is most often remembered for his statement that "Surely the Lord God will do nothing, but he revealeth his secret unto his servants the prophets" (Amos 3:7). There is safety in knowing that God always warns His people.

Isaiah—Perhaps the best known and certainly most quoted of all the Old Testament prophets is Isaiah. His name means *the Lord is Salvation.* Isaiah had great political influence as well as spiritual influence. He was a prophet to Judah for almost forty years from 740 BC to 701 BC.

Volumes have been written about Isaiah and he is quoted in all four standard works of The Church of Jesus Christ of Latter-day Saints. Even the Lord quoted Isaiah (3 Nephi 23:1) and commanded the people to search out and study his words.

Many people find it difficult to understand Isaiah. There are several reasons this may be the case.

1. Isaiah uses symbolism. When reading Isaiah, it is necessary to be prayerful so that the symbols can speak through the Holy Ghost.
2. Isaiah write in Hebrew poetic forms such as parallelism, inverted parallelism, and chiasmus, form of poetry when the ending lines reflect the opening lines, only in reverse order.
3. Isaiah writes for times other than his own, and his prophecies often have multiple layers of meaning. If you are wondering if he is talking about his time, the Savior's time, our time, or the Millennium, the answer is likely to be "yes!"

Nibbling at Isaiah will never do. A dedicated reader will prayerfully feast on the words of Isaiah and be spiritually filled.

Micah—Micah was the prophet during the reign of good King Hezekiah. He prophesied of the destruction of first Samaria and then Judah. He also prophesied about the Restoration. It is Micah to whom Herod turned to know that Messiah would be born in Bethlehem.

Nahum—His name means *consoler*. He prophesied around 642 BC. He prophesied about the fall of nations due to idolatry.

Zephaniah—His name means *the Lord hides*. He prophesied during the reign of good King Josiah, but he could see the terrible fate awaiting his people if they did not repent and turn away from evil.

Habakkuk—Like Isaiah, Habakkuk was a poet. He prophesied around the time of King Josiah or Jehoiakim, around 600 BC, just prior to the fall of Judah to Babylon. He questioned why a just God would punish His people for their wickedness using people who are even more wicked. God helped him to understand that God may allow wicked nations to "punish" Israel and Judah, but God will also, in time, "punish" the wicked nations.

Prophets to Judah during and after the Babylonian Exile

Jeremiah—He was born in a priestly family, so he must have been one of those from the House of Levi who had been scattered among all of Israel at the time of the Exodus. Jeremiah's prophecies and lamentations are difficult to read because he lived in such a dark time among self-deluded people who staggered from sin to sin like drunkards. He was called to preach to an already doomed people, so far lost to sin, that there was little hope of Jeremiah's preaching to change anyone's life. He was ridiculed, threatened, tortured and imprisoned. He preached for forty years from the time of King Josiah until after the final fall of Judah when Jerusalem and its temple were destroyed. Jeremiah was ultimately taken to Egypt where he died.

Ezekiel—Ezekiel was a priest of the Levitical priesthood and was called as a prophet in Babylon. His name means *God will strengthen*. He wrote about the resurrection and about the return of the Jews and the rebuilding of the temple. He it was who wrote about two sticks, on from Judah and one from Joseph (Ephraim) being one together at the last days. He is also remembered for his vision of the dry bones reassembling themselves in the resurrection.

Daniel—Daniel was one of the first Jews to be taken to Babylon. He was very bright and of the House of David (or royal descent). Three other young men were taken with him: Hananiah, Mishael, and Azariah (we know them best by the Babylonian names Shadrack, Meshack, and Abednego). Daniel, like Joseph, was blessed with the gift to interpret dreams. When Nebuchadnezzar had a troubling dream, he sent for all his wise men. He insisted that they tell him the dream and the interpretation thereof. The dream had gone from his head, but he remembered how troubling it had been. Of course, no one in the king's court could do it and the king was wroth. He threatened to put them all to death. Daniel stepped forward and proclaimed that he had a God in heaven who could reveal secrets. Daniel was given a night vision in which he saw the king's dream of an image of gold, silver, brass, iron, and clay mingled with iron. He said these represented the kingdoms of the world. The king also dreamed of a rock cut from a mountain without hands which rolled forward and grew until it destroyed the image. We believe that stone to be the gospel of Jesus Christ.

Haggai—He was a prophet after the return of the Jews. The people had been charged with rebuilding the gates of the city, but more importantly, to rebuild the temple. After several years, the people had rebuilt their own homes and had neglected the temple. Haggai gave them the Lord's admonition that they should be more concerned with rebuilding the temple than they were with making their own homes fancy. Haggai reminded them of their priorities.

Malachi—Malachi is the last book of the Old Testament, but Malachi was not the last prophet to Judah. His name means *my messenger*. His prophecies deal with the importance of marriage and the family as the cornerstone of the church and of society. He lamented that, because of sin, the people had forgotten. He prophesied that in the last days the hearts of the children would turn to their fathers.

Note

1. Many of the prophets in the Old Testament had syllables in their names that contained references to God's name. For example, in the name *Samuel*, the *el* refers to God, as in *Elohim*. Notice the *ah* in Jonah's name and the *iah* in Obadiah's name; both are references to Jehovah.

The Pride Cycle

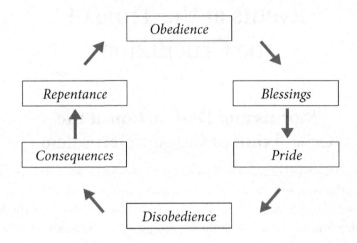

Choices within the Pride Cycle: Dealing with Cognitive Dissonance

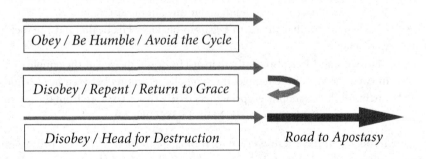

Geological and Astronomical Events at the Time of the Crucifixion

Storms and Destruction at the Crucifixion of Christ in Jerusalem

The actual gospel accounts of phenomena associated with the crucifixion comprise only two verses in Mark and three each in Matthew and Luke (Matthew 27:50–52; Mark 15:33, 37–38; Luke 23:44–46). So short are the references that it is easy to overlook them amongst all the information contained in those chapters. But there is a great deal of information contained in those eight verses.

These events associated with Jesus's death in Jerusalem began at the sixth hour around noon according to the timekeeping of the Jews.

- Mark and Luke testify that at the sixth hour, the sky began to darken; it stayed dark until the ninth hour, about three in the afternoon.
- Matthew writes that the earth began to quake at His death, and the rocks were rent.
- Matthew and Mark also testify that, at His death, the veil of the temple split in two. The veil of the temple, the symbolic separation between heaven and earth. All three synoptic gospel writers testify that it was torn from the top to the bottom (see Matthew 27:51; Mark 15:38; Luke 23).

In Herod's Temple there were two rooms, patterned after the rooms in Solomon's Temple and the Holy Tabernacle. The largest of the two was called the Holy Place and the smaller, the Holy of Holies. There, the Spirit of God dwelt. Only the high priest could enter, and then, only one day a year at Yom Kippur.[1] The rent veil represented that Christ had passed through the veil and, through the Atonement, made salvation available to all. According to Elder Bruce R. McConkie, "The Holy of Holies is now open to all, and all, through the atoning blood of the Lamb, can now enter into the highest and holiest of all places, that kingdom where eternal life is found."[2]

Storms and Destruction at the Crucifixion of Christ in the New World

I will now review the prophecies of the Lamanite prophet Samuel. He told of signs in the heavens that would signal Jesus's birth. Those signs appeared. He also prophesied of events that would herald the time of Jesus's death.

- The sun would be darkened, and the moon and stars would give no light for three days.
- There would be thunder and lightning for many hours.
- The earth would shake, and tremble and the rocks would be broken up, both on the surface of the earth and underneath the earth.
- There would be great tempests.
- Mountains would crumble, and new mountains would arise in some of the valleys.
- Cities would be destroyed, and roads would be broken up. (See Helaman 14.)

The geological and meteorological events that took place concurrent with the crucifixion were even more cataclysmic in the New World than in the Old. These events are chronicled in detail in 3 Nephi 8. They included:

- A great storm the like of which had never been seen before (no rain)
- Terrible thunder—never heard before
- Exceedingly sharp lightning—never seen before
- Shaking of the earth lasting three hours
- Some cities burning
- Other cities sunken into the sea
- Cities buried in the earth
- Whirlwinds
- Mountains where there had been none
- Rocks broken and seams and cracks upon on the face of the land
- Darkness over the face of the land for three days—a darkness that was felt as a vapor
- No light—sun, moon, or stars—for three days
- Darkness so heavy that no light could be kindled—no candle nor torch nor fire.
- Uncountable human misery—pain, injury, and death—great howling and mourning
- Radical changes in the topography of the land in its aftermath. (See 3 Nephi 8:5–23.)

On a Personal Note

A few years ago, I took a geology class at the local community college. It was hard work for my aging brain to learn it all, but learn I did. What I learned has strengthened my testimony of biblical and Book of Mormon accounts of events at the time of the crucifixion. (I strive to be a disciple first, then a scholar!)

To understand both accounts, it helps to understand the geological concept of *plate tectonics.* According to geologists, the crust of the Earth—the top layer—is not one solid, unbroken land mass. Rather, it is made up of a series of plates—looking like a huge jigsaw puzzle—that "float" on the Earth's mantle. The mantle itself is made of extremely hot, molten rock called *magma.* The heat of the magma causes the plates to move.

Where two plates come together, the movement of the magma causes the plates to do one of three things: they will pull apart; one will move under the other; or both will slide back and forth, each going in the opposite direction. The latter is called a *strike-slip boundary.* The places where tectonic plates come together are called *faults.* Any of the three movements described above can cause both earthquakes and volcanic eruptions.

I believe that the Bible records an earthquake sufficient in strength to rip a four-inch-thick veil and to disturb the hills surrounding Jerusalem such that it opened graves. There is a plate boundary to the east of the Mediterranean Ocean.

However, I believe that the Book of Mormon records volcanic eruption(s) with resultant earthquake(s) and tsunami(s). If the geographical area of the Book of Mormon covers southern Mexico, Guatemala, and Belize (as many LDS scholars believe), then it is a *hugely* volatile zone for volcanic activity. There is a strike-slip boundary of the Caribbean Plate and the North American Plate that runs along the northern borders of Guatemala, Belize, and Honduras. To the west, the North American Plate has a strike-slip boundary with the Cocas Plate near southern Mexico, and to the south, the Caribbean Plate bounds the South American Plate in El Salvador.[3]

One of the dangers around these multiple fault lines is that one seismic event can trigger another. We saw this recently in Japan when a second earthquake followed the first (a completely different quake, not an aftershock). Earthquakes and volcanic eruptions can also be related. A magnitude 4.2 earthquake in March of 1980 and a second 5.1 earthquake a few weeks later in May preceded the eruption of Mount St. Helens that same year.[4] Earthquakes can precede volcanoes and volcanoes can trigger earthquakes.

All the events described in 3 Nephi are geologically accurate representations of volcanic eruption. Here are some of the things that accompany large eruptions, particularly explosive eruptions that emit huge amounts of magma, ash, sulfur, gas, and pyroclastic "bombs" in a short amount of time:

- The heat of the magma superheating the air, causing great storms—violent wind, lightning, and thunder—but no rain
- Shaking in the earth that can last for hours (as opposed to the minute or two experienced in an earthquake)
- Great football-shaped pyroclastic "bombs" of hot lava bursting out with such force that they cause anything they touch to burst into flame
- Tornados
- Tsunamis that can wash away anything in their paths (remember Indonesia in 2004?)
- Massive amounts of lava extruded
- Earthquakes creating cracks and fissures in the earth
- New volcanic dome mountains
- Huge amounts of ash that can darken the skies for days (sometimes even weeks and months)
- Huge amounts of sulfur and other gas such that candles cannot be lit
- Massive devastation

The worst of these explosive volcanoes are called *super volcanoes.* They have such a volume of molten lava that they produce a massive eruption far move devastating that a normal eruption and spread that volume of lava over a wide area.[5] There is a large igneous province where the North American Plate, the Caribbean Plate, the Cocos Plate, the Panama Plate, and the North Andes Plate converge in Central America.[6]

Joseph Smith lived in nineteenth-century New York—not a volcanic zone. Little was known of the science of volcanology at that time (in fact, the concept of plate tectonics wasn't understood until the 1960s). If Joseph Smith wrote the Book of Mormon as critics claim, how could he have so accurately described volcanic destruction understood only within the last century?

The prophet Enoch saw in vision the crucifixion of Jesus. Moses wrote about it thus:

Enoch cried unto the Lord, saying: When the Son of Man cometh in the flesh, shall the earth rest? . . .

And the Lord said unto Enoch: Look, and he looked and beheld the Son of Man lifted up on the cross, after the manner of men; And he heard a loud voice, and the heavens were veiled; and all creations of God mourned; and the earth groaned; and the rocks were rent . . .

And again Enoch wept and cried unto the Lord, saying: When shall the earth rest? (Moses 7:54–56, 58)

The great Creator of heaven and earth was killed by His own people. Why wouldn't the earth groan and shake?

The Creator of the heavens and the earth was brutally put to death by His own people, and the earth wept. That groaning was reported in the Bible and the Book of Mormon. "Truly this man was the Son of God" (Mark 15:39).

There was no doubt that the Savior of the world had died.

Notes

1. Bruce R. McConkie, *New Testament Student Manual* (Church Educational System manual, 2014), 94.
2. *Doctrinal New Testament Commentary,* 3 vols. [1965–73], 1:830
3. Giacomo Corti, et al., "Active Strike-Slip Faulting in El Salvador, Central America," *Geological Society of America* 33, no. 12 (December 2005): 989, ftp://ftp.geology.wisc.edu/chuck/guatemala/References/Cortietal_ElSalv.pdf.
4. Mary Bagley, "Mount St. Helens Eruption: Facts & Information," *Live Science*, February 28, 2013, https://www.livescience.com/27553-mount-st-helens-eruption.html.
5. Scientists are currently researching super volcanoes at the European Synchrontron Radiation Facility in Grenoble, Switzerland. http://www.bbc.com/news/science-environment-25598050
6. "The Caribbean Plate," *Caribbean Tectonics*, accessed June 28, 2018, https://caribbean tectonics.weebly.com/caribbean-plate.html.

APPENDIX G

Secret Combinations

The term *secret combinations* is not found in the Bible, although it is common in the Book of Mormon. Having said that, evidence of secret combinations can be found throughout the Bible, from Cain to the crucifixion.

The LDS *Guide to the Scriptures* defines secret combinations in these words:

> An organization of people bound together by oaths to carry out the evil purposes of the group.[1]

We might say today that such people are part of a conspiracy. For example, evil men and women conspired in the assassinations of Presidents Lincoln and Kennedy. These conspiracies were, by definition, secret combinations.

We know from modern-day revelation that there have been secret combinations on earth since Cain.

> For, from the days of Cain, there was a secret combination, and their works were in the dark, and they knew every man his brother [other members of the combination.]
>
> [A descendant of Cain was Lamach.[2]] For Lamach having entered into a covenant with Satan, after the manner of Cain, wherein he became Master Mahan, master of that great secret which was administered unto Cain by Satan. (Moses 5:51, 49)

The Mahanic Principle, as I understand it, is "murder to get gain." It is when people subtly or openly covenant with Satan to get gain of any sort—money, power, political influence—through the heartless abuse of other people. When Cain entered a covenantal relationship with Satan to kill his brother, it was to gain his brother's flocks and wealth, but also to usurp his brother's position. When he did so, he was called Master Mahan.

People who choose God operate on the principle that one is to love people and use things to help others. People who choose Satan operate on a principle that is 180 degrees the opposite: one must love things above all else and use people to get them.

These are not people you should admire or try to emulate! Because of that, I don't want to dwell too much on the subject. I will just mention a few obvious examples.

- From the Old Testament: Cain slaying his brother; the plot to bring down Samson; plots to kill and silence multiple prophets, including Elijah and Isaiah.
- From the New Testament: the crucifixion—the plot to kill the Son of God.
- From the Book of Mormon: the Gadianton robbers, one of the most intricate and elaborate secret combinations recorded in scripture, they who were the organized crime groups of the ancient world.

Why is it necessary to even discuss such repulsive people and their lies? I include this short discussion because prophets have warned us that such conspiracies will and do exist today. Elder Lynn G. Robinson of the Seventy gave a devotional address at Brigham Young University in October of 2010. He explained to the students that as they enter the workforce to make a living, they should always keep their eternal goal of serving the Savior in mind. He wrote:

> The motives that drive people are the hinges upon which major outcomes swing. The Lord has identified two opposite motivators—God and mammon [see 3 Nephi 12:24]. We know that money itself is not evil; in fact, it represents "the sweat of [our] face." Mammon goes beyond money to "the love of money," which is referred to as "the root of all evil." (See 1 Timothy 6:10).

He went on to describe six levels of motives from complete love of the Lord to complete lust for Satanic wealth and power. The worst of these levels is what Elder Robbins called *F Level,* the one in which secret combinations lie. He said:

> Many at the F level may be identified at the D level [lusting for filthy lucre at any cost] but actually fit better here because of their negative impact on communities and nations. At this level, we find those who don't contribute but only take—through organized crime, Internet scams, Ponzi schemes, and so forth. At this level, you have murder and elimination of competition. Secret combinations, which Moroni said would be a real threat in our day [see Ether 8:24], operate at this level.[3]

We hear of these groups everywhere today. Avoid them like the plague! I am concerned when I see so many good men and women being led astray by "get rich quick" schemes that lead them down the path of exploiting others for gain.

Enough said: to be forewarned is to be forearmed.

Notes

1. Guide to the Scriptures, "Secret Combinations," scriptures.lds.org.
2. If I counted the generations correctly, Cain was Lamach's sixth-great-grandfather.
3. Lynn G. Robbins, "Making a Living, Making a Life," *Ensign*, December 2013.

Witnesses to the Literal Resurrection of Jesus Christ

L et us look at witnesses' testimonies recorded in the Bible: those who saw and heard Jesus and those who saw, heard, and touched Him.

Witness(es)	Biblical Reference
Witnesses who saw and heard Him	
Apostles	Luke 24:36–49
Two disciples on the road to Emmaus	Luke 24:30, 31
Five hundred of the brethren	1 Corinthians 15:8
Apostle Paul	1 Corinthians 15:8
Witness who saw, heard, and touched Him	
Apostle Thomas	John 20:24–29
The women at the tomb	Matthew 28:9
Mary Magdalene	John 20:11, 14–17

APPENDIX I

Old Testament Genealogy from Adam to Abraham

Adam*
Seth
Enos
Cainan
Mahalaleel
Jared
Enoch*
Methuselah
Lamech
Noah*
Shem
Arphaxad
Salah
Eber
Peleg
Reu
Serug
Nahor
Terah
Abraham*

* Patriarch of a
Dispensation

APPENDIX J

Kings and Prophets in Israel and Judah

Kings	ISRAEL'S KINGS:	Jeroboam	Omri	Ahab
Saul				
David	ISRAEL'S PROPHETS:		Elijah	Elisha
Solomon				
	JUDAH'S KINGS:	Asa	Rehoboam	**Jehoshaphat**
Samuel				
Nathan	JUDAH'S PROPHETS:			
	Jeremiah			
Prophets				

Bold:
Righteous Kings

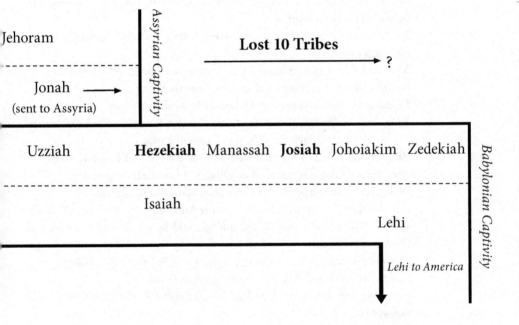

The Fate of Jesus's Original Apostles

One by one, the Apostles and other righteous priesthood leaders were martyred. Here are some whose fates are known:

- James, son of Zebedee and brother of John, was the first martyred Apostle, beheaded by Herod Agrippa.
- Matthew was executed, probably by beheading, in Ethiopia, where he was serving a mission.
- Matthias, who replaced Judas Iscariot, was stoned to death in Jerusalem.
- Andrew, brother of Peter, was crucified on an X-shaped cross, probably in Macedonia. The cross became known as St. Andrew's Cross.[1]
- Peter was crucified in Rome. Tradition says that he claimed to be unworthy of a death like the Savior's, so he was crucified upside down.
- Paul was beheaded in Rome about AD 65 at the order of Emperor Nero.
- Simon the Zealot was crucified in a Roman province in England.
- Philip was crucified by the Emperor Domitian, also upside down.
- Bartholomew was martyred, possibly near Armenia. One account said he was severely beaten and crucified and another said he was placed in a sack and thrown into the sea.
- Thomas preached as far east as India and was killed there by a lance.
- James, the brother of Matthew, was stoned in Jerusalem.
- Barnabus, the first Seventy and missionary companion to Paul, was killed in Cyprus.
- John, brother of James and son of Zebedee, often called John the Beloved, was banished to a penal colony on the Isle of Patmos by the Emperor Domitian. He was later released and returned to his home in Ephesus. The ancient historian Hippolytus wrote that "he fell asleep at Ephesus, where his remains were sought for but could not be found."[2] Scripture tells us that John did *not* die, but was translated to remain upon the earth until the Savior comes again (John 21:22–23; D&C 7:1–3).

Notes

1. The flag of Scotland has an X-shaped white cross on a blue field and is known as St. Andrew's Cross.
2. Scott R. Peterson, *Where Have All the Prophets Gone?* (Springville, UT: Cedar Fort Publishing, 2005), 115–117.

APPENDIX L

The Sermon on the Mount and the Sermon at the Temple

Jesus Christ taught the people of Nephi in in what has come to be known as the Sermon at the Temple. This is found in 3 Nephi 12, and I mention it here because it is such a vital testimony of the reality of Jesus Christ and the consistency of His gospel. If you read it, you will notice a couple of important things.

First, the sermon is similar to, but not exactly like, that found in Matthew, and it follows a logical progression of steps that define entering into a Christian life. Many modern Biblical scholars feel that the Sermon on the Mount was merely a collection of assorted sayings over time that the writers of the gospels cobbled together. The Sermon at the Temple lays that argument in the dust. It is a cohesive, single sermon.

Next, you will notice a small change in wording that has great significance. In the Sermon on the Mount, Jesus refers His listeners to the altar of the temple; for example, from Matthew 5:23–24:

> Therefore if thou bring thy gift to the altar, and there rememberest that thy brother hath ought against thee;
> Leave there thy gift before the altar, and go thy way; first be reconciled to thy brother, and then come and offer thy gift.

Now read the sermon from 3 Nephi 12:23–24:

> Therefore, if ye shall come unto me, or shall desire to come unto me, and rememberest that they brother hath aught against thee—
> Go thy way unto thy brother, and first be reconciled to thy brother, and then come unto me with full purpose of heart, and I will receive you.

In the Biblical version, Jesus directed his disciples to the altar of temple, the place of sacrifice. In the Book of Mormon, He directs them to Himself, having fulfilled the Law of Moses and ended sacrifice by the shedding of blood.

Finally, at the end of both sermons, Jesus commands His followers to be *perfect*. But in the Bible, it says be perfect like the Father is perfect; in the

Book of Mormon, it says be perfect like both He and the Father are perfect. In the Hebrew culture and language, the word *perfect* means complete, integrated, whole. In Judea, Jesus was at the beginning of His mortal ministry with the Atonement, crucifixion, and resurrection still ahead of Him. His mission wasn't yet complete. But in Bountiful, He was speaking as the resurrected Lord whose mission was complete and, therefore, perfect. The sermon is a beautiful outline of the steps of discipleship, from recognizing our spiritual poverty through walking in His footsteps toward perfection.

Some years ago, a non-LDS scholar was asked, as part of a project at Brigham Young University, to compare and contrast the two sermons. When presenting his findings, this PhD of Religious Studies said that in Judah, Jesus was teaching as a rabbi, not much different from many other rabbis of His day. But in Bountiful, Jesus was teaching as a God.[1] This is a *huge* difference and is found consistently throughout the sermon. For example, the 3 Nephi account frequently includes the words "come unto me." Here are just a few examples from the Beatitudes. I have italicized the differences where they occur and underlined the key phrases.

Sermon on the Mount: Matthew 5, KJV	Sermon at the Temple: 3 Nephi 12
Blessed are the poor in spirit: for theirs is the kingdom of heaven.	*Yea,* blessed are the poor in spirit *who come unto me* for theirs is the kingdom of heaven.
Blessed are they that <u>mourn</u>: for they shall be <u>comforted</u>.	*And again,* blessed are *all* they that <u>mourn</u>, for they shall be <u>comforted</u>.
Blessed are the <u>meek</u>: for they shall inherit the <u>earth</u>.	*And* blessed are the <u>meek</u>, for they shall inherit the <u>earth</u>.
Blessed are they which do <u>hunger</u> and <u>thirst</u> after <u>righteousness</u>: for they shall be filled.	*And* blessed are *all* they who do <u>hunger</u> and <u>thirst</u> after <u>righteousness</u>, for they shall be <u>filled</u> *with the Holy Ghost.*
Blessed are the <u>merciful</u>: for they shall obtain mercy.	*And* blessed are the <u>merciful</u>, for they shall obtain mercy.
Blessed are the <u>pure</u> in <u>heart</u>: for they shall <u>see</u> God.	*And* blessed are all the <u>pure</u> in <u>heart</u>, for they shall <u>see</u> God.
Blessed are the <u>peacemakers</u>: for they shall be called the <u>children</u> of God.	*And* blessed are *all* the <u>peacemakers</u>, for they shall be called the <u>children</u> of God.

Ye are the <u>salt</u> of the earth: but if the salt have lost his savour, wherewith shall it be salted? it is thenceforth good for nothing, but to be cast out, and to be trodden under foot of men.	*Verily, verily, I say unto you, I give unto you to be* the salt of the earth; but if the <u>salt</u> shall lose its savor wherewith shall *the earth* be salted? *The salt shall* be thenceforth good for nothing, but to be cast out and *to be* trodden under foot of men.
Ye are the <u>light</u> of the world. A city that is set on an hill cannot be hid.	*Verily, verily, I say unto you, I give unto you to be* the <u>light</u> of this people. A city that is set on a hill cannot be hid.
Neither do men light a <u>candle</u>, and put it under a bushel, but on a candlestick; and it giveth light unto all that are in the house.	Behold, do men light a <u>candle</u> and put it under a bushel? *Nay*, but on a candlestick, and it giveth light to all that are in the house;
Let your <u>light</u> so shine before men, that they may see your good <u>works</u>, and glo<u>rify</u> your Father which is in heaven.	*Therefore* let your <u>light</u> so shine before *this people*, that they may see your good <u>works</u> and <u>glorify</u> your Father *who* is in heaven.
Think not that I am come to <u>destroy</u> the <u>law</u>, or the prophets: I am not come to destroy, but to fulfil.	Think not that I am come to <u>destroy</u> the <u>law</u> or the prophets. I am not come to destroy but to fulfil; *And behold, I have given you the law and the commandments of my Father, that ye shall believe in me, and that ye shall repent of your sins, and come unto me with a <u>broken heart</u> and a contrite spirit. Behold, ye have the commandments before you, and the <u>law</u> is fulfilled.* *Therefore <u>come</u> unto me and be ye saved; for verily I say unto you, that except ye shall keep my <u>commandments</u>, which I have commanded you at this time, ye shall in no case enter into the kingdom of heaven.*[2]
Ye have heard that it was said by them of old time, Thou <u>shalt</u> not <u>kill</u>; and whosoever shall kill shall be <u>in</u> danger of the judgment:	Ye have heard that it **hath been** said by them of old time, **and it is also written before you, that** thou <u>shalt</u> not <u>kill</u>, and whosoever shall kill shall be <u>in</u> danger of the judgment *of God*.

But I say unto you, That whosoever is <u>angry</u> with his brother ***without a cause*** shall be in danger of the judgment:[3]	But I say unto you, that whosoever is <u>angry</u> with his brother shall be in danger of his judgment.
Therefore if thou bring thy gift to the ***altar***, and there remember that thy brother hath ought against thee; leave there thy gift before the ***altar***, and go thy way; first be reconciled to thy brother, and then come and offer thy gift.	Therefore, if ***ye shall come unto me, or shall desire to come unto me,*** and remember that thy brother has ought against thee—go thy way *unto thy brother, and* first be reconciled to thy brother, and then ***come unto me with full purpose of heart, and I will receive you.***
Ye have heard that it was said by them of old time, Thou shalt not commit <u>adultery</u>:	***Behold, it is written*** by them of old time, that thou shalt not commit <u>adultery</u>;
But I say unto you, That whosoever <u>looketh</u> on a <u>woman</u> to <u>lust after</u> her hath committed <u>adultery</u> ***with her*** already in his heart.	But I say unto you, that whosoever <u>looketh</u> on a <u>woman</u>, to <u>lust after</u> her, hath committed <u>adultery</u> already in his heart.
Ye have heard that it hath been said, Thou shalt <u>love</u> thy <u>neighbor</u>, and hate thine enemy.	***And behold it is written also,*** that thou shalt <u>love</u> thy <u>neighbor</u> and hate thine enemy;
But I say unto you, Love your <u>enemies</u>, bless them that curse you, do <u>good</u> to them that hate you, and <u>pray</u> for them which despitefully use you, and persecute you. That ye <u>may be</u> the <u>children</u> of your Father which is in heaven: ***For if ye love*** them which love you, what reward have ye? do not even the publicans the same? ***And if ye salute your brethren only, what do ye more than others?*** do not even the publicans so?[4]	But ***behold*** I say unto you, love your <u>enemies</u>, bless them that curse you, do <u>good</u> to them that hate you, and <u>pray</u> for them ***who*** despitefully use you and persecute you; That ye <u>may be</u> the <u>children</u> of your Father ***who*** is in heaven; ***Therefore those things which were of old time, which were under the law, in me are all <u>fulfilled</u>.*** ***Old things are done away, and all things have become <u>new</u>.***[5]
Be ye therefore perfect, even as your Father which is in heaven is perfect.	***Therefore, I would that ye should be*** perfect even as ***I,*** *or* your Father ***who*** is in heaven is perfect.

Notes

1. Gaye Strathearn in *Messiah: Behold the Lamb of God*.

2. This is a clear explanation about what it means to say that Christ fulfilled the law. He also here makes a direct reference to the new law of sacrifice being that of a broken heart and a contrite spirit rather than the shedding of an animal's blood. This is indicative of His teaching as a God and not a rabbi.

3. Who has lashed out in anger and not felt—at least in the moment of anger—that his anger was justified? This, I believe, is a scribal error. I don't think Jesus told people they could have license to rage (and I think that is the anger He is talking about) if they had a good cause.

4. Prior to Christ's Atonement, crucifixion, and resurrection, the law of Moses was still in force. The laws of Rome were also a heavy burden on the Jews. Jesus spent a lot of time telling His followers that if they were sued for their coat, they should give their cloak also. If they were compelled to walk a mile (a Roman could compel a Jew to walk a mile with him and carry his burdens for him), they were to walk two. He was teaching them to reach a little higher. A slave must walk one mile. A free man may choose to walk the extra mile. All of this was in preparation for the fulfillment of the law, which was fulfilled in Him.

5. Jesus is very explicit again in teaching that the old "eye for an eye" law has been fulfilled in Him and that old things are now made new. He taught his followers in Judea that one doesn't put new wine in old bottles. The New Testament and Covenant of His flesh and blood were not a patch on the Law of Moses, as many of the Judaizers would like to suppose, but an entirely new relationship with the Lord where the law was written on the fleshy tablets of their hearts and not upon tablets of stone.

ACKNOWLEDGMENTS

S pecial thanks to my dear friend Bonnie Patricia Peplow for her insight, wisdom, and questions.

Gracious gratitude to my granddaughter Caite Marie Buntin for catching the jots and tittles.

—KATHLEEN RAWLINGS BUNTIN DANIELSON, Spring 2018

ABOUT THE AUTHOR

Kathleen Rawlings was born in 1944 in Provo, Utah. She began writing when she was a young child, taking after her great-grandfather whom she called Poppy. She grew up in a show business family in Las Vegas, Nevada, and has two sisters, Darlene Rawlings Richards and Nancy Rawlings, and one brother, Brent Rawlings.

Kathleen was always a curious child. *Why do I have to go to bed? What makes rain? Why is the sky blue?* Her parents, G. Barney and Hazel P. Rawlings, encouraged her to read and study. When she was nine years old, she and her best friend decided they wanted to read the Bible. They didn't make it further than Genesis, but her fascination for the Old Testament began there. She read every children's book she could find on the subject, trying to bridge together the chronology of the stories she heard in Primary about men like Noah and Jonah and Adam.

She loved hearing the stories about Jesus when she was young, and out of that grew a love for the New Testament. By the time she was seventeen, she had read and studied the Book of Mormon. Taking Moroni's challenge (Moroni 10:4–5) she gained an unswerving testimony of the book.

As an adult, she continued her scripture reading and loved to study using Institute study guides and commentaries on the scriptures.

She was married to the late Carmon Buntin for twenty years until his death in 1982. She and Carmon are the parents of four children, grandparents of fourteen grandchildren, and great-grandparents of twelve—at last count—great-grandchildren. Following Carmon's death, Kathleen worked for twenty years in Mesa, Arizona, as a teacher, counselor, and district administrative specialist. She retired in 2002.

She remarried in 2004 and moved to Snowflake, Arizona, with her husband Richard. Following the death of her second husband in 2008, she served a full-time mission in the Church Office Building at Church Headquarters in Salt Lake City, where she spent eighteen months as the Global Communications Manager for the Church-Service Missionary Department.

In 2012, she was called out of retirement by a group of local parents. Because of that meeting, she co-founded a charter school, George Washington Academy, with her business partner, State Senator Sylvia Allen. She continued to serve as principal before retiring again in 2016.

Since retiring, she has moved to Gold Canyon, Arizona, to be near family. She focuses most of her time on her writing, including her blog, drkathyscouchthereprise.blogspot.com, and her most recent book, *A Pig in the Kitchen*, written about her life with her husband and children on a mini-farm in Gilbert, Arizona.

She loves working out with her trainer and swimming several days a week. She is still fascinated to learn new things about the gospel. She loves teaching in the Church and sharing her testimony in her writing. She has served in a variety of callings in the Church. She is a popular public speaker and teacher.

Scan to visit

drkathyscouchthereprise.blogspot.com